Good Guys, Bad Guys, and Sidekicks in Western Movies

From the 1930's through the 1960's

Gary Koca

GOOD GUYS, BAD GUYS, AND SIDEKICKS IN WESTERN MOVIES

Copyright © 2016 Gary Koca

All rights reserved.

ISBN-13: 978-1537282794
ISBN-10: 1537282794

FORWARD

Westerns were a huge part of movies during the silent movie era and even more so beginning in the late 1930's through the 1960's. Westerns developed such great stars as John Wayne, Gary Cooper, and Randolph Scott, and were instrumental in the careers of movie luminaries like James Stewart, Henry Fonda, Alan Ladd, Glenn Ford, and Clint Eastwood. Stars not normally associated with westerns - like Burt Lancaster, Gregory Peck, Robert Taylor, and Joel McCrea - also made a number of quality westerns.

However, after the 1960's, westerns dropped out of sight for several decades as movie westerns fell out of favor with the baby boomers. After all, we had more relevant concerns than what took place in the American west after the Civil War – Vietnam, social unrest, civil rights, equality, and women's rights were just some of those issues that movies seemed to focus on. Who needed westerns with good guys and bad guys clearly differentiated?

But in recent years, westerns have made somewhat of a comeback. Films like *Unforgiven* (Oscar winner for Best Picture), *Tombstone*, *Dances with Wolves* (another Best Picture Oscar winner), *Open Range*, and *Silverado* have brought a renaissance to the western, truly the most American form of films. Even an old west comedy like *Blazing Saddles* has helped bring the western film back into the limelight.

Therefore, this book will concentrate on my personal favorites in three categories of westerns[1]:
1. Good Guys (and one gal)
2. Bad Guys and Sidekicks
3. My all-time favorite western films – again, my own personal favorites.

---

[1] I have selected stars and films that are MY personal favorites. I am not claiming that they are necessarily the best western films of those stars, however.

GOOD GUYS, BAD GUYS, AND SIDEKICKS IN WESTERN MOVIES

This book is dedicated to all fans of classic western movies from the 1930's to the 1960's. Not the serials, not the "B" westerns with stars like Roy Rogers, Gene Autry, Hopalong Cassidy's William Boyd, and Buck Jones, just to name a few; and not the great television shows like The Lone Ranger, The Cisco Kid, Gunsmoke, Bonanza, or others. As good as those shows were, this book has a specific movie, not television, focus.

CONTENTS

Forward – Good Guys

Section One – Good Guys (and gal)

1	John Wayne	2
2	James Stewart	23
3	Gary Cooper	36
4	Randolph Scott	50
5	Henry Fonda	64
6	Glenn Ford	78
7	Richard Widmark	90
8	Gregory Peck	105
9	Burt Lancaster	115
10	Barbara Stanwyck	127

NOTE: Clint Eastwood would certainly be in with this group, but his best westerns started in the mid 60's, not really the era of focus of this book. But otherwise, he would certainly deserve to be included.

SECTION ONE – GOOD GUYS

One thing that is clear about the vast majority of westerns of that era is that the good guys were always really good and the bad guys always really bad. You knew from the outset who was the hero and who was the villain. So this section of the book is dedicated to those individuals who were almost always the good guys in their films. For each individual, I have included a short biography followed by a collection of 3-10 of my favorite westerns that star was involved with. The good guys include the following:

1. John Wayne.
2. James Stewart
3. Gary Cooper
4. Randolph Scott
5. Henry Fonda
6. Glenn Ford
7. Richard Widmark
8. Gregory Peck
9. Burt Lancaster
10. Barbara Stanwyck

While they weren't always the good guy – Glenn Ford in *The Man from Colorado* and *3:10 to Yuma*, Henry Fonda in *Once Upon a Time in the West*, Gregory Peck in *Duel in the Sun*, Burt Lancaster in *Vera Cruz*, and Richard Widmark in several roles – they generally played the part of the hero rather than the villain in the vast majority of their films.

1. JOHN WAYNE – 1907-1979

The number one star in my book is, of course, John Wayne. The Duke was the the ultimate western hero, and probably the number one hero of World War II movies to boot. He had a profound effect on Hollywood and American films from his first starring role in 1930 until his last film in 1976 – a career of over 46 years! If you ask anyone under the age of 30 to name one classic film star from the 1930's through 1950's, they would probably pick John Wayne.

In spite of the general notion that Wayne was not much of an actor, he was actually pretty darn good in many of his films. His best performance was not the one he received an Oscar for, *True Grit*, but more likely *The Searchers* (shown above), *Red River*, or *The Sands of Iwo Jima*; and three of these four movies are westerns. Other better than average John Wayne westerns include *The Man Who Shot Liberty Valance* (also starring James Stewart), the cavalry trilogy of *Fort Apache*, *She Wore a Yellow Ribbon*, and *Rio Grande*, *3 Godfathers*, and *Hondo*.

My favorite John Wayne westerns are for the most part, the ones I just mentioned:

1. The Searchers
2. Red River
3. Hondo
4. The Man Who Shot Liberty Valance
5. She Wore a Yellow Ribbon
6. Fort Apache
7. 3 Godfathers
8. Angel and the Badman
9. Rio Bravo
10. Stagecoach

BIOGRAPHY

Actor John Wayne was born Marion Robert Morrison on May 26, 1907, in Winterset, Iowa. (Some sources also list him as Marion Michael Morrison and Marion Mitchell Morrison.) A larger than life character in American movies, he was already a sizable presence when he was born, weighing around 13 pounds.

The older of two children born to Clyde and Mary "Molly" Morrison, Wayne moved to Lancaster, California, around the age of seven. The family moved again a few years later after Clyde failed in his attempt to become a farmer.

Settling in Glendale, California, Wayne received his distinctive nickname "Duke" while living there. He had a dog by that name, and he spent so much time with his pet that the pair became known as "Little Duke" and "Big Duke," according to the official John Wayne website. In high school, Wayne was a good student and was involved in many different activities, including student government and football. (I can picture him bashing the liberals in debate, even at 18.) He also participated in numerous student theatrical productions.

Winning a football scholarship to the University of Southern California (USC), Wayne started college in the fall of 1925. He joined the Sigma Chi fraternity and continued to be a strong student. (That means he was in the same fraternity at the same time as another Hollywood leading man, Buster Crabbe, who starred in the *Flash Gordon* serials from 1936 through 1940.). Unfortunately, after two years, an injury ended his football career and ended his scholarship, forcing him to leave college since his family was hardly wealthy. While in college, Wayne had done some work as a film extra, appearing as a football player in *Brown of Harvard* (1926) and *Drop Kick* (1927).

Western Star

Out of school, Wayne worked as an extra and a prop man in the film industry. He first met director John Ford while working as an extra on *Mother Machree* (1928). With *The Big Trail* (1930), Wayne received his first leading role, thanks to director Raoul Walsh. Walsh is often credited with helping him create his now legendary screen name, John Wayne. Unfortunately, the western was a box office dud, and it almost ended the career of John Wayne before it got off the ground.

For nearly a decade, Wayne toiled in numerous B movies-mostly westerns-for different studios as well as serials such as *Hurricane Express* and *Shadow of the Eagle*, both made in 1932. He even played a singing cowboy named Sandy Saunders among his many roles. During this time period of B westerns and serials, however, Wayne started developing his man of action persona, which would serve as the basis of many popular characters later on.

Working with his mentor John Ford, he got his next big break in *Stagecoach* (1939). Wayne portrayed the Ringo Kid, an escaped outlaw, who joins an unusual assortment of characters on a dangerous journey through frontier lands. During the trip, the Kid falls for a dance hall prostitute named Dallas (Claire Trevor). The film was well received by movie goers and critics alike and earned seven Academy Award nominations, including one for Ford's direction. In the end, it took home the awards for Music and for Actor in a Supporting Role for Thomas Mitchell. You may remember Mitchell as Scarlett O'Hara's father in *Gone with the Wind*.

Around this time, Wayne made the first of several movies with German actress and famous sex symbol Marlene Dietrich. The two appeared together in *Seven Sinners* (1940) with Wayne playing a naval officer and Dietrich as a woman who sets out to seduce him. Off-screen, they became romantically involved, though Wayne was married at the time. There had been rumors about Wayne having an occasional affair (certainly not many by Hollywood standards at the time), but nothing as substantial as his connection to Dietrich.[2] Even after their physical relationship ended, the pair remained good friends and co-starred in two more films, *Pittsburgh* (1942) and *The Spoilers* (1942).

John Wayne - Action Hero

Wayne started working behind the scenes as a producer in the late 1940s. The first film he produced was *Angel and the Badman* (1947). Over the years, he operated several different production companies, including John Wayne Productions, Wayne-Fellows Productions, and Batjac Productions.

Wayne's career as an actor took another leap forward when he worked with director Howard Hawks in *Red River* (1948). The western drama provided Wayne with an opportunity to show his talents as an actor, not just an action hero. Playing the conflicted cattleman Tom Dunson, he took on a darker sort of character. He deftly handled his character's difficult relationship with his adopted son, played by Montgomery Clift. Also around this time, Wayne received praise for his work in John Ford's *Fort Apache* (1948) with Henry Fonda and Shirley Temple.

Taking on a war drama, Wayne gave a strong performance in *Sands of Iwo Jima* (1949), which garnered him his first Academy Award nomination for Best Actor. He also appeared in two more westerns by Ford now considered classics: *She Wore a Yellow Ribbon* (1949) and *Rio Grande* (1950) with Maureen O'Hara.

---

[2] Wayne said that Marlene Dietrich was the best lover he ever had.

Wayne worked with O'Hara on several films, perhaps most notably *The Quiet Man* (1952). Playing an American boxer with a bad reputation, his character moved to Ireland where he fell in love with a local woman (Maureen O'Hara). This film is considered Wayne's most convincing leading romantic role by many critics.

Politics and Later Years

A well-known conservative and anticommunist, Wayne merged his personal beliefs and his professional life in 1952's *Big Jim McLain*. He played an investigator working for the U.S. House Un-American Activities Committee, which worked to root out communists in all aspects of public life. Off screen, Wayne played a leading role in the Motion Picture Alliance for the Preservation of American Ideals and even served as its president for a time. The organization was a group of conservatives who wanted to stop communists from working in the film industry; other members included Gary Cooper and some fellow with higher political aspirations named Ronald Reagan. I will say that his films dealing with communism – including *The Green Berets* – were generally not among his best.

In 1956, Wayne starred in another Ford western, *The Searchers*,[3] and again showed some dramatic range as the morally questionable Civil War veteran Ethan Edwards. He then reteamed with Howard Hawks for *Rio Bravo* (1959). Playing a local sheriff, Wayne's character faced off against a powerful rancher and his henchmen who want to free his jailed brother. The unusual cast included Dean Martin, Walter Brennan, singing star Ricky Nelson, and Angie Dickinson.[4]

Wayne made his directorial debut with *The Alamo* (1960). Starring in the film as Davy Crockett, he received decidedly mixed reviews for both his on- and off-screen efforts. (It was probably too much to ask

---

[3] My personal vote for his best film and best performance

[4] This film was basically remade as *El Dorado* in 1966, this time with Robert Mitchum in the Dean Martin role.

him to play producer, director, and star in such a huge effort. Richard Widmark, for one, would definitely attest to that. Wayne and Widmark did not get along at all on the set, especially since Widmark was a liberal Democrat.) Wayne received a much warmer reception for *The Man Who Shot Liberty Valance* (1962) with Jimmy Stewart and Lee Marvin and directed by John Ford. Some other notable films from this period include *The Longest Day* (1962) and *How the West Was Won* (1962). Continuing to work steadily, Wayne refused to even let illness slow him down. He successfully battled lung cancer in 1964. To defeat the disease, Wayne had to have a lung and several ribs removed.

In the later part of the 1960s, Wayne had some great successes and failures. He co-starred with Robert Mitchum in the previously-mentioned *El Dorado* (1966) and with Kirk Douglas in *The War Wagon* (1967), which were both well received. The next year, Wayne again mixed the professional and the political with the pro-Vietnam War film *The Green Berets* (1968). He directed and produced as well as starred in the film, which was derided by critics for being heavy handed and clichéd (as well as overly optimistic about the U.S. presence in Vietnam). Viewed by many as a piece of propaganda, the film still did well at the box office.

Outside of film work, Wayne continued to espouse his conservative political views. He supported good friend Ronald Reagan in his 1966 bid for governor of California as well as his 1970 re-election effort. In 1976, Wayne recorded radio advertisements for Reagan's first attempt to become the Republican presidential candidate.

Wayne also won his only Academy Award for Best Actor for *True Grit* (1969). He played Rooster Cogburn, a one-eyed drunkard and lawman, who helps a young woman named Mattie (Kim Darby) track down her father's killer. Rounding out the cast was Glenn Campbell as a young Texas Ranger; Robert Duvall and Dennis Hopper were among the bad guys the trio had to defeat. While this film was not necessarily the Duke's best performance, it was in a sense a career achievement Oscar.

Death and Legacy

Wayne portrayed an aging gunfighter dying of cancer in his final film, *The Shootist* (1976), with Jimmy Stewart and Lauren Bacall. His character, John Bernard Books, hoped to spend his final days peacefully, but got involved in one last gunfight. In 1978, life imitated art with Wayne being diagnosed with stomach cancer.

Wayne died on June 11, 1979, in Los Angeles, California. He was survived by his seven children from two of his three marriages. During his marriage to Josephine Saenz from 1933 to 1945, the couple had four children, two daughters - Antonia and Melinda - and two sons - Michael and Patrick. Both Michael and Patrick followed in their father's footsteps: Michael as a producer and Patrick as an actor. With his third wife, Pilar Palette, he had three more children: Ethan, Aissa, and Marisa. Ethan has worked as an actor over the years.

Shortly before his death, the U.S. Congress approved a congressional gold medal for Wayne. Both Elizabeth Taylor and Maureen O'Hara testified before Congress and passionately endorsed Wayne for the award. It was given to his family in 1980. In the same month as the Duke's passing, the Orange County Airport was renamed after him. He was later featured on a postage stamp in 1990 and again in 2004 and was inducted into the California Hall of Fame in 2007.

In honor of his charitable work in the fight against cancer, Wayne's children established the John Wayne Cancer Foundation in 1985. The organization provides support to numerous cancer-related programs and to the John Wayne Cancer Institute at Saint John's Health Center in Santa Monica, California.[5]

---

[5] Located in Santa Monica, California. The John Wayne Cancer Institute was founded in 1981, two years after the death of John Wayne. Its specialties are treatment of cancer and also research into the causes of caner.

While Wayne was a conservative, he was also a good listener and would willingly listen to another person's point of view, unlike his close friend Ward Bond. [6]

AWARDS AND RECOGNITION

Among his many awards the following stand out:
- Three Oscar nominations – for best actor for *The Sands of Iwo Jima* (1949) and *True Grit* (1969 – for which he won the Oscar – and as producer for *The Alamo* in 1960
- Three Golden Globe awards, for *True Grit* as well as the Cecil B. DeMille award in 1966 and the Henrietta Award in 1960
- Two Golden Apple awards for most cooperative actor
- Four People's Choice awards as most popular actor – 1975, 1976, 1977, and 1978. 1975 was the first year of the award, so

---

[6] According to the Eyman biography, you could not be in a Ward Bond movie unless you passed his political litmus test, which meant being an extreme right wing conservative.

Wayne won the award its first four years.
- 13 Laurel Award nominations, of which he won six[7]
- Four Western Heritage Awards
- Congressional Gold Medal recipient - 1979

MY FAVORITE JOHN WAYNE WESTERNS

1. *The Searchers* - 1956

The Searchers may simply be John Wayne's best film and best acting performance. He displays a range of character not typically found in Wayne films – a basically good man with anger management issues, to say the least.

Returning from the Civil War to the Texas ranch of his brother, Ethan Edwards hopes to find a home with his family and to be near the woman he obviously but secretly loves – his brother's wife. But a Comanche raid destroys these plans, and Ethan sets out, along with his 1/8 Indian nephew Martin (Jeffrey Hunter), on a years-long journey to find the niece kidnapped by the Indians under Chief Scar as well as the murderers of her older sister. But as the quest goes on,

---

[7] This award was created by *Motion Picture Exhibitor* magazine, and ran from 1957 to 1968, then 1970 and 1971.

Martin begins to realize that his uncle's hatred for the Indians is beginning to spill over onto his now-indoctrinated niece. Martin becomes uncertain whether Ethan plans to rescue Debbie..or kill her when and if he finds her.

The film co-stars Vera Miles, Ward Bond, Natalie Wood as the niece, and Henry Brandon as Chief Scar. A collection of John Wayne regulars also appear in the movie, including Harry Carey, Jr. and Hank Worden. In an early 1990's interview, Steven Spielberg said that this movie was possibly the greatest film of all time, due to the depth of the character studies. That might be a bit of an exaggeration, but it is certainly one of the greatest western films ever made. And it really did not do all that well at the box office when it was first released, perhaps because it did not meet the expectations of the typical John Wayne persona.

Henry Brandon, pictured here as Chief Scar, had a long Hollywood career. At 6'5", he was one of the few actors who was taller than John Wayne at 6'4 ½". Generally cast as the villain, he appeared in *Babes in Toyland* with Laurel and Hardy and was the evil Captain Laska in the 1939 serial *Buck Rogers* with Buster Crabbe cast as Rogers.

2. *Red River* - 1948

Again, John Wayne turns in a good performance in a film based on the first cattle drive along the Chisholm Trail from Texas to Abilene, Kansas. He begins as a young man in his early 30's and for most of the film plays a hardened cattle owner in his late 40's.

Fourteen years after starting his cattle ranch in Texas with only two steers, Tom Dunston is finally ready to drive his 10,000 head of cattle to market. Back then Dunston, his sidekick Nadine Groot (Walter Brennan) and a teen-aged boy, Matt Garth (a very young Montgomery Clift) who was the only survivor of an Indian attack on a wagon train. The nearest market, however, is in Abilene, Kansas, which is 1000 miles away. Dunston is a hard task master demanding a great deal from the men who have signed up for the drive.

The stubborn Dunston won't listen to advice from anyone and alienates virtually everyone on the drive, including Matt and Groot. Soon, the men on the drive are taking sides and Matt ends up in charge with Dunston vowing to kill him. Red River ends, of course, in a fight between father and stepson and includes many exciting moments along the way.

Also in the cast are Joanne Dru, John Ireland (the two were married in 1949), Noah Berry, Jr. and Harry Carey Sr. and Jr.

3. *Hondo* – 1953

Next page. John Wayne as Hondo – vintage John Wayne at his best!

GOOD GUYS, BAD GUYS, AND SIDEKICKS IN WESTERN MOVIES

While *Hondo* is certainly not his best film, it may be John Wayne's most representative film. He plays a loner who finds the love of a woman and her young son, and protects them from all sorts of potential disasters.

Hondo Lane, a dispatch rider for the cavalry, encounters Angie Lowe (Geraldine Page in a good role), a woman living alone with her young son in the midst of hostile Apache territory. She presumes she is safe because the Apaches, under their chief Vittorio, have always left them alone. Later Lane has a run-in with Angie's worthless husband and is forced to kill him, not knowing at the time who he is. Vittorio captures Lane and to save his life, Angie tells the Apache chief that Lane is her husband, unaware that Lane has killed her real husband. In order to protect her from a forced marriage with one of the young Apache warriors, Lane reluctantly goes along with the lie, though he knows the truth must eventually come out, to both Vittorio and Angie.

This representative John Wayne western also includes Ward Bond, Michael Pate, Leo Gordon, and a young James Arness.

Professional basketball player John Havlicek bore such a close resemblance to John Wayne that his nickname was Hondo through his career. You be the judge.

GOOD GUYS, BAD GUYS, AND SIDEKICKS IN WESTERN MOVIES

4. *The Man Who Shot Liberty Valance* – 1962

When Senator Ransom Stoddard (James Stewart) returns home to Shinbone for the funeral of his former friend Tom Doniphon (John Wayne), he recounts to a local newspaper editor the story behind it all. He had come to town many years before, a lawyer by profession. The stage was robbed on its way in by the local thug, Liberty Valance (a very mean and thoroughly nasty Lee Marvin), and Stoddard has nothing left save a few law books. So he gets a job in the kitchen at the Ericson's restaurant and there meets his future wife, Hallie – at that time, Wayne's girlfriend.

The territory is vying for Statehood and Stoddard is selected as a representative over Valance, who continues terrorizing the town. When Valance destroys the local newspaper office and attacks the editor, Stoddard calls him out, though the conclusion is not quite as straightforward as legend would have it. As Stewart says at the very end of the film, "This is the west, sir. When the legend becomes fact, print the legend."

An extremely strong supporting cast includes Vera Miles as the love interest of the two stars, Edmond O'Brien, Andy Devine, Woody Strode, and John Carradine, among others. This is also one of those movies where John Wayne actually says "Pilgrim" – in fact, he says it many times.

5. *She Wore a Yellow Ribbon* - 1949

One of the three films in the John Ford-directed cavalry trilogy. On the verge of his retirement at Fort Starke, a one-troop cavalry post, aging U.S. Cavalry Captain Nathan Cutting Brittles (John Wayne) is given one last mission: to take his troop and deal with a breakout from the reservation by the Cheyenne and Arapaho following the defeat of George Armstrong Custer at the Battle of the Little Big Horn.

Brittles' task is complicated by being forced at the same time to deliver his commanding officer's wife Abby Allshard (Mildred Natwick) and niece, Olivia Dandridge (the beautiful Joanne Dru), to an eastbound stage, and by the need to avoid a new Indian war. His troop officers, 1st Lt. Flint Cohill (John Agar) and 2nd Lt. Ross Pennell (Harry Carey, Jr.), meanwhile vie for the affections of Miss Dandridge while uneasily anticipating the retirement of their captain and mentor.

Assisting him with his mission is Capt. Brittles' chief scout, Sgt. Tyree (Ben Johnson), a one-time Confederate cavalry officer; his first sergeant, Quincannon (Victor McLaglen), and Maj. Allshard (George O'Brien), Brittles' long-time friend and commanding officer.

After apparently failing in both missions, Brittles returns with the troops to Fort Starke to retire. His lieutenants continue the mission in the field, joined by Brittles after "quitting the post and the Army". Unwilling to see more lives needlessly taken, Brittles takes it upon himself to try to make peace with Chief Pony That Walks (Chief John Big Tree). When that too fails, he devises a risky stratagem to avoid a bloody war by stampeding the Indians' horses out of their camp, forcing the Indians to return to their reservation. The movie ends with Brittles being recalled to duty as chief of scouts with the rank of Lt. Colonel and Miss Dandridge and Lt. Cohill becoming engaged.

McLaglen was very good as Wayne's first sergeant. John Agar, by the way, was related to the Agar Ham family; he was married to Shirley

GOOD GUYS, BAD GUYS, AND SIDEKICKS IN WESTERN MOVIES

Temple for five years, and was a conservative, all of which certainly made him compatible with Wayne.

John Agar, star of countless B horror films in the 50's plus westerns and war films, and like John Wayne, a conservative.

6. *Ft. Apache* – 1948

1948 was a really good year for John Wayne, with him starring in *Red River*, *Ft. Apache*, and **3 Godfathers** – the next film – as well as the non-western *Wake of the Red Witch* that year. *Ft. Apache* was the first film in the John Ford cavalry trilogy group, the third being *Rio Grande*.

Ft. Apache is less of an uplifting look at western heroes than the previous Ford film. Here, Ford slowly reveals the true character of Owen Thursday (an outstanding performance by Henry Fonda), who sees his new posting to the desolate Fort Apache as a chance to claim the military honor which he believes is rightfully his. Arrogant and obsessed with military form over substance, Thursday attempts to destroy the Apache chief Cochise after luring him across the border from Mexico, against the advice of his subordinates, in particular John Wayne as Captain Kirby York.

Accompanying widower Thursday to his new post is his daughter, Philadelphia (Shirley Temple). She becomes attracted to Second Lieutenant Michael Shannon O'Rourke (John Agar again), the son of Sergeant Major Michael O'Rourke (Ward Bond). While Agar is a

West Point graduate and an officer, the class-conscious Thursday forbids his daughter to see someone he does not consider a gentleman.

When there is unrest among the Indians, led by Cochise, Thursday ignores York's advice to treat the natives with honor and to focus instead on problems caused by corrupt Indian agent Silas Meacham. Thursday's inability to deal with Meacham effectively, due to his rigid interpretation of Army regulations stating that Meacham is an agent of the United States government and therefore entitled to Army protection (despite his own personal contempt for the man), coupled with Thursday's prejudicial and arrogant ignorance regarding the Apache, drives the Indians to rebel. Eager for glory and recognition, Thursday orders his regiment into battle on Cochise's terms, which means a direct charge into the hills, despite York's urgent warnings that such a move would be suicidal. Of course, York is correct.

Ford's casting of Fonda as less than totally honorable and the emphasis on the native American point of view make this film a true western classic. Having both Fonda and Wayne in the film is a real plus, and the two actors work well together. A good supporting cast includes Wayne regulars Agar, Victor McLaglen, and Ward Bond, as well as Grant Withers as the crooked Indian agent, and Miguel Inclan as Cochise.

7. *3 Godfathers* - 1948

John Wayne, Pedro Armendáriz and Harry Carey Jr. (one of his first roles) are bank robbers on the run, saddled with an infant they have promised to care for to its dying mother. They plunge into desperate times as they flee across the Arizona desert. (The film was actually filmed in Death Valley, California.)

3 Godfathers is somewhat of a takeoff on the three wise men Christmas story theme, with the three men vowing to save the child, no matter what happens – even death. That fact adds a nice touch to a good western. All the other actors play very minor roles in this film, released in December of 1948 (not surprisingly).

8. *Angel and the Badman* - 1947

This little-known gem is actually one of my favorite John Wayne westerns, mostly because of the chemistry between Wayne and co-star Gail Russell. Quirt Evens (John Wayne) is an all-around tough guy, maybe not a bad person but certainly with a checkered and criminal past. As the film begins, Quirt is wounded and on the run; he manages to ride onto a farm owned by Quaker Thomas Worth and his family and promptly collapses from exhaustion.

The daughter, Penelope Worth (Gail Russell) immediately sees something of value in him, and personally takes charge of nursing Quirt back to health. During the recovery period, she explains to him the Quaker code of non-violence and what it means to her. It is clear that there is an obvious attraction between Quirt and Penelope, in spite of her Quaker values and his reputation as a gunman.

After recovering, Quirt decides to stay on and help the family with chores as a farmhand. He actually helps end a feud peacefully between Thomas Worth and a neighbor over water rights, and receives a Bible at a Quaker gathering for his help in settling the dispute in a peaceful way. More and more, Quirt is now torn between his violent past and the non-violent ways of the Quakers and the woman he has come to love.

The rest of the film demonstrates this struggle between Quirt attempting to begin a new life while being tempted by his past.

Throughout this entire period, the local marshal – played by veteran Western actor Harry Carey - warns Quirt that he is the wrong man for Penny and will inevitably wind up at the end of a rope. Quirt's old adversaries appear and cause a situation in which Penny is injured and clinging to life. Quirt decides to exact his revenge against the two gunmen. Does he, or doesn't he? You will have to view the film!

9. *Rio Bravo* - 1959

Rio Bravo is another John Wayne buddy western, and was essentially remade as *El Dorado* in 1966.

The sheriff of a small town in southwest Texas – Wayne as John T. Chance - must keep custody of a murderer whose brother, a powerful rancher, is trying to help him escape. After a friend is killed trying to muster support for him, he and his deputies - a disgraced drunk (Dean Martin) and a cantankerous old guy who hobbles around (Walter Brennan) - must find a way to hold out against the rancher's hired guns until the marshal arrives. In the meantime, matters are complicated by the presence of a young gunslinger (Ricky Nelson, believe it or not) - and a mysterious beauty (Angie Dickenson) who just came in on the last stagecoach.

Rio Bravo is a good buddy movie with lots of action, a good plot, and a small group of good guys against bad guys with superior numbers. The chemistry between the three male leads – Wayne, Martin, and Brennan – is good, and Dean Martin is pretty believable as the drunken deputy. Ricky Nelson as a cowboy is a bit of a stretch, and a 25-year-old Angie Dickenson falling for the 59-year-old Wayne is also a reach. But all in all, things move quickly in this film, and John Wayne is the essence of the western hero in this film. Also included in the cast are Wayne regulars Ward Bond and Harry Carey, Jr., as well as John Russell and Claude Akins.

10. *Stagecoach* – 1939

Stagecoach is the film that rescued John Wayne from a career of B movies and serials and made him a star. It is also the first of many

John Ford westerns that is set in Monument Valley on the Arizona-Utah border.

In 1880, an assorted group of strangers boards the east-bound stagecoach from Tonto, Arizona Territory to Lordsburg, New Mexico Territory. These travelers appear unremarkable and ordinary at first glance. Among them are Dallas (Claire Trevor), a prostitute who is being driven out of town by the members of the women's "Law and Order League"; an alcoholic doctor, Doc Boone (Thomas Mitchell); pregnant Lucy Mallory (Louise Platt), who is traveling to see her cavalry officer husband; whiskey salesman Samuel Peacock (Donald Meek); gambler and Southern gentleman Hatfield (John Carradine); and local banker Henry Gatewood (Berton Churchill), who we know is making a quick getaway with $50,000 in funds stolen from his bank.

When the stagecoach driver, Buck (Andy Devine), looks for his normal shotgun guard, Marshal Curly Wilcox (George Bancroft) tells him that the guard has gone searching for a fugitive, the Ringo Kid. Buck tells Marshal Wilcox that Luke Plummer (Tom Tyler) is in Lordsburg (their destination). Knowing that Kid has vowed to avenge the deaths of his father and brother at Plummer's hands, the marshal decides to ride along as guard. As they set out, U.S. cavalry Lieutenant Blanchard (Tim Holt) informs the group that Geronimo and his Apaches are on the warpath and his small troop will provide an escort until they reach Dry Fork.

Along the way, they come across the Ringo Kid (John Wayne), whose horse became lame and left him without transportation. Even though they are friends, Curly has no choice but to take Ringo into custody. As the trip progresses, Ringo takes a strong liking to Dallas.

When the stage reaches Dry Fork, the group is informed that the expected cavalry detachment has gone to Apache Wells. Buck wants to turn back, but Curly demands that the group vote. With only Buck and Peacock objecting, they decide to proceed on to Apache Wells. At lunch before departing, the group is taken aback when Ringo invites Dallas to sit at the main table, and Mrs. Mallory is clearly uncomfortable having lunch with a prostitute. When they arrive in Apache Wells, Mrs. Mallory goes into labor when she hears that her husband had been wounded in battle. Doc Boone is called upon to assist the delivery, and later Dallas emerges holding a healthy baby girl. Later that night, Ringo asks Dallas to marry him. A bit later, Ringo escapes but returns when he sees smoke signals as signs of an Apache attack. The passengers quickly gather their belongings and leave to avoid any encounters with the Apache.

When the stagecoach reaches Lee's Ferry, the passengers find that the station and ferry have been burned and those who were not killed have fled. Curly releases Ringo from his handcuffs just as they are attacked by Apaches. During a long chase, Peacock and Buck are hit and they all run out of ammunition. As Hatfield is about to use his last bullet to save Mrs. Mallory from being taken alive, he is fatally wounded. Just then, the 6th U.S. cavalry arrives to the rescue of the group. The stage does arrive in Lordsburg with the rest of the group intact. Does Curly exact his revenge against the Plummers? Does Curly return to jail or does he marry Dallas? You will have to watch the movie to find out.

Stagecoach won Oscars for Best Supporting Actor – Thomas Mitchell – and Best Music. It was nominated for Best Picture, Best Director, Best Cinematography, Best Art Direction, and Best Film Editing. It lost out for Best Picture to a film you may have heard of – *Gone with the Wind*.

Previous page. George Bancroft, John Wayne as the Ringo Kid, and Claire Trevor realize they are in danger of being attacked by Indians.

SUMMARY

John Wayne was a true Hollywood icon and probably the best-known western star in movie history. He holds the record for most leading roles by an actor – 142, a record that is likely to never be equaled. While he made films in many other genres, he is certainly best known for the great westerns he made. I have focused on only ten of them, but there probably could have been at least another ten worth mentioning.

2. JAMES STEWART – 1908-1997

While James Stewart made a wide variety of films, including comedies, dramas, sports movies, and war movies, he also starred in many outstanding westerns throughout his long career which lasted from 1934 through 1991. Regardless of the type of film, Stewart typically played honest, average middle class individuals who are unwittingly drawn into some kind of conflict or crisis.

My favorite James Stewart westerns are the following:
1. Winchester '73
2. The Man Who Shot Liberty Valance
3. Destry Rides Again
4. Bend of the River
5. The Naked Spur
6. The Man from Laramie
7. Firecreek

BIOGRAPHY

One of film's most beloved actors, Jimmy Stewart made more than 80 films in his lifetime. He was known more than just about any movie star of his generation for his everyman quality, which made him both appealing and accessible to audiences. Stewart grew up in the small town of Indiana, Pennsylvania, where his father operated a hardware store. (Not surprising that an "everyman" film star would be the son of a guy who owned a hardware store.)

Stewart got his first taste of performing during his time as a young man. At Princeton University, he acted in shows as a member of the Triangle Club.. Stewart earned a degree in architecture in 1932, but he never practiced the trade. Instead he joined the University Players in Falmouth, Massachusetts, the summer after he graduated. There Stewart met fellow actor Henry Fonda, who became a lifelong friend. (Two great friends despite the fact that Fonda was a dedicated Democrat while Stewart was definitely a conservative Republican.)

That same year, Stewart made his Broadway debut in *Carrie Nation*. The show didn't fare well, but he soon found more stage roles. In 1935, Stewart landed a movie contract with MGM and headed out west.

Early Films

In his early Hollywood days, Stewart shared an apartment with Henry Fonda. The tall, lanky 6'3" actor appeared in a number of films – including *After the Thin Man*, where he was the murderer - before co-starring with Eleanor Powell in the 1936 popular musical comedy *Born to Dance*. Another career breakthrough came with Frank Capra's *You Can't Take It With You* (1938). This comedy won an Academy Award for Best Picture, and made Stewart a star.

Stewart also played the lead in Capra's *Mr. Smith Goes to Washington* (1939). In this film, he portrayed a young, idealistic politician who takes on corruption. Stewart received his first Academy Award nomination for this film. The following year, he won an Oscar for the wonderful romantic comedy *The Philadelphia Story*. Stewart co-starred with Katharine Hepburn and Cary Grant in this terrific film.

Later Career

From 1941 to 1946, Stewart took a break from his acting career to serve in World War II. He joined the U.S. Army Air Corp (later known as the U.S. Air Force) and rose up through the ranks to become a colonel by war's end. In 1946, Stewart returned to the big screen with *It's a Wonderful Life* directed by Frank Capra. The movie was a disappointment at the box office, but it has since become a Holiday favorite over the years. Stewart reportedly considered it to be one of his favorite films.

Stewart went on to star in *Harvey* (1950), a humorous movie about a man with an imaginary rabbit for a friend. But he seemed to be less interested in doing this type of lighthearted film in his later career. Stewart sought out grittier fare after the war, appearing in Anthony Mann's westerns *Winchester '73* (1950) and *Broken Arrow* (1950). He also became a favorite of director Alfred Hitchcock, who cast him in several thrillers. They first worked together on *Rope* (1948). *Vertigo* (1958) is considered by many to be Hitchcock's masterpiece and one of Stewart's best performances. The following year, Stewart also won rave reviews for his work in Otto Preminger's *Anatomy of a Murder*.

Final Years

In the 1970s, Stewart made two attempts at series television. He starred on *The Jimmy Stewart Show*, a sitcom, which ran from 1971 to 1972. The following year, he switched to drama with *Hawkins*. Stewart played a small-town lawyer on the show, which proved to be short-lived. Around this time, he also made a few film appearances. For example, Stewart worked opposite John Wayne, Lauren Bacall and Ron Howard in the 1976 western *The Shootist*.

Stewart became the recipient of numerous tributes during the 1980s for his substantial career. In 1984, Steward picked up an honorary Academy Award "for his high ideals both on and off the screen." By the 1990s, Stewart had largely stepped out of the public eye. He was deeply affected by the death of his wife Gloria in 1994. The couple had been married since 1949 and had twin daughters together. He also became a father to her two sons from a previous marriage. Jimmy and Gloria Stewart were one of Hollywood's most enduring couples, which only added to his reputation as an upstanding and honorable person.

Poor health plagued Stewart in his final years. He died on July 2, 1997, in Beverly Hills, California. While he may be gone, his movies have lived on and inspired countless other performers.

AWARDS AND RECOGNITION

Among James Stewart's many awards are the following:
- Stewart was nominated for five Best Actor Oscar awards: *Anatomy of a Murder*, *Harvey*, *It's a Wonderful Life*, *The Philadelphia Story*, and *Mr. Smith Goes to Washington*, and won the Oscar for *The Philadelphia Story*.
- Stewart also won an honorary Oscar in 1985 for "his fifty years of memorable performances, for his high ideals both on and off the screen, with respect and affection of his colleagues.
- He was nominated for four Golden Globe awards, including two for television
- Nominated for 13 Laurel Awards, and won two of those outright.[8]
- Lifetime achievement award from the Screen Actors Guild in 1969.

MY FAVORITE JAMES STEWART WESTERNS

1. *Winchester '73* – **1950**

---

[8] The Laurel Awards were cinema awards to honor films, actors, actresses, directors and composers. This award was created by *Motion Picture Exhibitor* magazine, and ran from 1957 to 1968, then 1970 and 1971.

Lin McAdam (James Stewart) and his pal High Spade (Millard Mitchell) compete for a valued Winchester rifle. McAdam wins the shooting contest, but the rifle is immediately stolen by the runner-up, Dutch Henry Brown (Stephen McNally), a notorious outlaw. This "story of a rifle" then follows McAdams' pursuit, and the rifle as it changes hands, until a final showdown and shoot-out on a rocky mountain precipice.

Lin and High Spade encounter a whole variety of characters, including Shelley Winters, John McIntire, and Dan Duryea (naturally as a psychotic villain named Waco Johnny Dean – it should have been Wacko Johnny Dean). Rock Hudson and Tony Curtis, in the beginning of their careers, also appear in minor roles.

While Stewart was always good as the typical noble western hero, Winchester '73 changed the way cinema audiences saw the western and Stewart, because it featured a more complex idea of the noble hero of the west -- a man plagued by personal problems and some violent impulses.

James Stewart and the Winchester '73 of the title

2. *The Man Who Shot Liberty Valance* - 1962

This film was already profiled under John Wayne, so I will abbreviate the summary here. When Senator Ransom Stoddard (James Stewart) returns home to Shinbone for the funeral of his former friend Tom Doniphon (John Wayne), he recounts to a local newspaper editor the story behind it all.

The territory is vying for Statehood and Stoddard is eventually selected as a representative over outlaw Liberty Valance, who continues terrorizing the town. When Valance destroys the local newspaper office and attacks the editor, Stoddard has had enough. Eventually, Valance meets his end and Stewart, not Wayne, gets the girl. I guess this proves that even in the Old West, a man of letters can compete with a man of action.

The climax of Liberty Valance – from left, John Wayne, James Stewart, and Lee Marvin to the right. Who shot Valance?

3. *Destry Rides Again* - 1939

Destry Rides Again is a classic western with a different message – Destry does not use a gun to solve problems. This original version of this film starred James Stewart and Marlene Dietrich. There was also a 1954 remake with Audie Murphy and even a 1959 musical with Andy Griffith as Destry. But the first version was clearly the best.

Kent (Brian Donlevy), the unscrupulous boss of Bottleneck has Sheriff Keogh killed when he asks one too many questions about a rigged poker game that gives Kent a stranglehold over the local cattle ranchers. The mayor, who is in cahoots with Kent, appoints the town drunk, Washington Dimsdale (Charles Winninger, who was Abel Frake in the 1945 version of *State Fair*), as the new sheriff, assuming that he'll be easy to control. But what the mayor doesn't know is that Dimsdale was a deputy under famous lawman Tom Destry, and is able to call upon the – he thinks - equally formidable Tom Destry, Jr to be his deputy. But this Tom Destry is a very, very low key guy who does not use a gun. The theme of the film is how he surprises the townspeople by turning up to be the opposite of what they think he is – a coward.

Dietrich has a few great musical numbers – my own favorite is "See What the Boys in the Back Room Will Have" - and brings a lot to the film. But the most fun is really Stewart, whenever he wants to make a statement he gives the audience an example of several fictitious friends. Also, Dietrich's Frenchie was certainly the inspiration for Madeline Kahn's *Blazing Saddles* character, Lili Von Schtupp.

Marlene Dietrich as Frenchie – the original dance hall singer, at least in *Destry Rides Again*.

Madeline Kahn as Lili Von Schtupp – a takeoff on Dietrich's character from *Destry Rides Again*. She even spoke with a thick German accent in *Blazing Saddles*.

4. *Bend of the River* - 1952

Bend of the River is an under-rated western featuring a good performance by Stewart and an even better one by Arthur Kennedy. Two men with questionable pasts, Glyn McLyntock (Stewart) and his friend Emerson Cole (Kennedy), lead a wagon-train load of homesteaders, including Cole's fiancée and her father (Julie Adams and Jay C. Flippen) from Missouri to the Oregon territory. They establish a settlement outside of Portland and as winter nears, it is necessary for McLyntock and Cole to rescue and deliver food and supplies to the settlement, upriver and over a mountain. During the trip, Cole double crosses his best friend by engineering a mutiny to divert the supplies to a gold mining camp for a handsome profit.

Stewart and Kennedy are teamed up well and make a good buddy team, then adversaries.

Julie Adams' most famous film role was as the love interest of the creature in the original *Creature from the Black Lagoon*. The creature really had good taste! Adams is still alive as of the writing of this book. She makes an occasional appearance on "Svengoolie" on Me-TV when Sven shows that film.

5. *The Naked Spur* - 1953

Another good James Stewart western with an outstanding cast featuring Robert Ryan, Janet Leigh, Ralph Meeker, and Millard Mitchell (again, as Stewart's buddy as in *Winchester '73*.) Howard Kemp (Stewart) is a bounty hunter who's been after killer Ben Vandergroat (Ryan) for a long time. Along the way, Kemp is forced to take on a couple of partners, an old prospector named Jesse Tate (Mitchell) and a dishonorably discharged Union soldier, Roy Anderson (Meeker). When they learn that Vandergroat has a $5000 reward on his head, greed starts to take the better of them. Vandergroat takes every advantage of the situation sowing doubt between the two other men at every opportunity and finally convincing one of them to help him escape. Vandergroat also uses his reluctant girlfriend (Leigh) in a plan to escape from Kemp.

Stewart gives his usual good performance, but Robert Ryan steals the show as the scheming killer. The climax of the film takes place at the bend of the river – hence, the title.

6. *The Man from Laramie* - 1955

Mysterious Will Lockhart, a guy with a past he does not want to talk about (James Stewart) delivers supplies to storekeeper Barbara Waggoman (Cathy O'Donnell) at Coronado, an isolated town in Apache country. Before long, he's tangled with Dave Waggoman (Alex Nicol), vicious son of autocratic rancher Alec (Donald Crisp) and cousin of nice girl Barbara. The ranch foreman (Arthur Kennedy again) is Will's best friend, and they work together to keep Dave in tow. Will thinks about leaving but sticks around town, his presence a catalyst for changes in people's lives, while searching for someone he doesn't know...someone who's been selling rifles to the Apaches.

The film is not a simple western oater but has lots of meaty dialogue and adult themes. The cast is very good, with Stewart, Crisp, Arthur Kennedy (always good) and Cathy O'Donnell as Barbara. Some characters are better than they seem and at least one is much worse than we initially believe. But Stewart is good in a role that tests his acting talents.

If you are wondering where you saw Cathy O'Donnell before,

she played Ben Hur's sister in the Charlton Heston version of the film. She was also Harold Russell's girlfriend in *The Best Years of Our Lives*, perhaps my all-time favorite film.

7. *Firecreek* – 1968

Firecreek is a late 1960's western featuring a 60-year-old James Stewart pitted against Henry Fonda (in real life, Stewart's best friend.)

Johnny Cobb (Stewart) moonlights as a $2 a month sheriff in the quiet little western town of Firecreek. When a gang of thugs passes through, their leader Larkin (Fonda), who is suffering from a minor wound, decides the gang needs to spend the night. The gang members prove to be vicious, sadistic sociopaths who take advantage of the frightened townspeople, humiliating them for their own perverse amusement. Although Larkin disapproves of their behavior, his leadership role is tenuous, and he is reluctant to test it by exercising control over his men. The mild-mannered Cobb, really a farmer more than a lawman, also is reluctant to challenge the gang, hoping that they will just go away the next morning. Things come to a head when Meli, an Indian woman with a mixed race child, is sexually attacked by one of vicious psychopaths. Arthur, a mentally-challenged stable boy, comes to her aid and accidentally kills her attacker. Cobb locks up Arthur pending a trial, but when the sheriff visits his pregnant wife, the gang breaks into the jail and lynches the boy. Cobb realizes that he will have to deal with the gang, most likely without any help from the townspeople.

Stewart brings a real vulnerability to the role of the sheriff. He is a reluctant hero, and would just prefer that the gang have their fun and be gone the next morning. Fonda is in charge of a bunch of psychos, and not a bad guy himself, but he hesitates taking a stand against the violence and brutality of his gang. Definitely an adult western, Firecreek features a solid cast that includes Gary Lockwood, James Best, and Jack Elam as other gang members, and Inger Stevens, Dean Jagger, Jay C. Flippen, Barbara Luna, and Ed Begley as some of the townspeople.

I just can't imagine that many women in the old West looked like Inger Stevens. She played in several westerns, including *Firecreek* and *Hang 'Em High*, with Clint Eastwood, but tragically committed suicide with an overdose of pills at the age of 35.

> James Stewart and Henry Fonda were best buddies off the screen. They roomed together when they first got to Hollywood. After that, they got together regularly at each other's homes and enjoyed working on model airplanes together, often without saying a word for an entire day. Stewart was a conservative republican and Fonda a liberal Democrat, but that never seemed to interfere with their friendship.

Best friends – Stewart and Fonda – they worked on model airplanes together, but probably never discussed politics.

SUMMARY

While James Stewart made his mark in films as kind of an everyman in several areas, his greatest impact may well have been in westerns. And he played in some pretty good ones throughout his career, as you can see. A very good actor, and an even better person.

3. GARY COOPER – 1901-1961

It's really a tossup on my all-time favorite western star. Certainly, the list of John Wayne's hits is impossible to beat. But there is something about Gary Cooper as a heroic western figure that no one else can match.

It's hard to think of an actor of the era who was more well liked by his peers, both female and male. For example, of all the leading men that Jean Arthur was paired up with – including James Stewart, Cary Grant, Ronald Colman, William Holden, Alan Ladd, and Joel McCrea, just to name a few – Gary Cooper was her favorite. Whether as a western hero, a war hero like Sergeant York, a baseball player like Lou Gehrig, or an everyman like Longfellow Deeds or John Doe, he always turned in a believable performance and never over-acted. Even those co-workers who thought that Cooper wasn't working all that hard were amazed to see how, in the final product, Cooper was actually out-acting everyone else, albeit in a subtle, unobtrusive manner. And, for the purposes of this book, he made a number of great westerns.

My favorite Gary Cooper westerns are the following:
1. High Noon – big surprise here!
2. The Westerner
3. Sergeant York
4. Vera Cruz
5. The Plainsman
6. Along Came Jones
7. Friendly Persuasion

Gary Cooper's movie career stretched all the way from silent films into the 1950s. He won an Academy Award for his portrayal of Alvin York in *Sergeant York*.

BIOGRAPHY

Early Life

Actor Gary Cooper (real name was Frank Cooper) was born on May 7, 1901, in Helena, Montana. Spanning from the silent film era to the early 1960s, Academy Award-winning actor Gary Cooper built much of his career by playing strong, manly, distinctly American roles. The son of English parents who had settled in Montana, he was educated in England for a time. Injured in an auto accident while attending Wesleyan College, he convalesced on his dad's Montana ranch, perfecting the riding skills that would see him through many a future Western film.

He also studied at Grinnell College in Iowa before heading to Los Angeles to work as an illustrator. After trying to make a living at his chosen avocation as an illustrator of political cartoons, Cooper was encouraged by two friends to seek employment as a cowboy extra in movies. But agent Nan Collins felt she could get more prestigious work for the handsome, gangling Cooper, and, in 1926, she was instrumental in obtaining for the actor an important role in *The Winning of Barbara Worth*. At first, Coop couldn't really act at all, but he applied himself to his work in a brief series of silent Westerns for his home studio, Paramount Pictures, and, by 1929, both his acting expertise and his popularity had soared.

Then his career began to take off. He starred opposite silent movie star Clara Bow in *Children of Divorce* (1927). Another key early performance was a supporting role in *Wings* (1927) as a pilot. Cooper also earned praise as the ranch foreman in *The Virginian* (1929), one of his early films with sound, where he was cast as The Virginian; in this film he developed the reserved, concise speech patterns that became fodder for every impressionist on radio, nightclubs, and television for the next 30 years.

Throughout the 1930s, he turned in a number of strong performances in such films as *A Farewell to Arms* (1934) with Helen Hayes and *Mr. Deeds Goes to Town* (1936) directed by Frank Capra. Cooper received an Academy Award nomination for his work on the film. He had a very good performance as the baseball player-turned-everyman in *Meet John Doe*, with Barbara Stanwyck in 1941, one of my own favorite Gary Cooper films, since I am a huge baseball and Chicago Cub fan.

An American Hero Playing American Heroes

Cooper continued to excel on the big screen, tackling several real-life dramas. In *Sergeant York* (1941), he played a World War I hero and sharpshooter, which was based on the life story of Alvin York. Cooper earned a Best Actor Academy Award for his portrayal of York. The real Alvin York would only consider doing a film on his life if Gary Cooper portrayed him.

The next year, Cooper played one of baseball's greats, Lou Gehrig, in *The Pride of the Yankees* (1942). When Eleanor Gehrig, Lou's wife, saw the film, she said that Cooper had picked up Lou's mannerisms perfectly. In 1943, appearing in a film adaptation of Ernest Hemingway's *For Whom the Bell Tolls*, Cooper starred opposite Ingrid

Bergman in a drama set during the Spanish Civil War. These two performances garnered him his third and fourth Academy Award nominations. Too old for World War II service, Cooper gave tirelessly of his time in hazardous South Pacific personal-appearance tours.

In 1952, Cooper took on what is considered his signature role as Will Kane in *High Noon*. He appeared as a lawman who must face a deadly foe without any help from his own townspeople. The film won four Academy Awards, including a Best Actor win for Cooper.

Personal Life and Death

In addition to his excellent on-screen performances, Cooper became known for his alleged romances with several of his leading ladies, including Clara Bow and Patricia Neal. The affair with Neal, his co-star in 1949's *The Fountainhead*, reportedly occurred during his marriage to socialite Veronica Balfe with whom he had a daughter. Their marriage seemed to survive the scandal.

Working mostly in Westerns by the 1950s (including the classic *High Noon*), Cooper was yet able to retain his box-office stature in his 50's. Privately, however, he was plagued with painful, recurring illnesses, and one of them developed into lung cancer. By the late 1950s, Cooper's health was clearly in decline. He only made a few more films, such as *Man of the West* (1958).

Gary Cooper received an honorary Oscar at the 1961 Academy Awards for his long and successful career in films but was too ill to attend the ceremony, so his close friend James Stewart accepted the Honorary Oscar on his behalf. Stewart's emotional speech hinted that something was seriously wrong, and the next day newspapers ran the headline, "Gary Cooper has cancer." One month later, on May 13, 1961, six days after his 60th birthday, Cooper died, a victim of cancer.

AWARDS AND RECOGNITION

Gary Cooper was nominated for five Academy Awards for Best Actor and won two. (Frankly, he could easily have won all five.)

He won for:
- *Sergeant York* – 1941
- *High Noon* – 1952

He was nominated for
- *Mr. Deeds Goes to Town* – 1936
- *The Pride of the Yankees* – 1942
- *For Whom the Bell Tolls* – 1943

Cooper was also given an honorary Oscar in 1961 for "his many memorable screen performances and the international recognition he, as an individual, has gained for the motion picture industry."

Cooper also won Golden Globes for *High Noon* and *Friendly Persuasion* and won four Laurel Awards.

MY FAVORITE GARY COOPER WESTERNS

1. *High Noon* - 1952

On the day he gets married and hangs up his badge, lawman Will Kane (Gary Cooper) is told that a man he sent to prison years before, Frank Miller, is returning on the noon train to exact his revenge. Having initially decided to leave with his new spouse (the beautiful Grace Kelly), and despite his new wife's views to the contrary, Will decides he must go back and face Miller and his gang. However, when he seeks the help of the townspeople he has protected for so long, one by one they turn their backs on him. Their excuses vary:
1. I'm too old – former sheriff Lon Chaney, Jr.
2. We're no match for them – the townspeople
3. It's not our fight, they are only after the Sheriff
4. I would gladly help if there were other volunteers
5. Go ahead and leave so I can be the sheriff – deputy sheriff Lloyd Bridges

The only one who really volunteers to help with no strings attached is a young boy, who Sheriff Kane spares from the battle.

It seems Kane may have to face Miller and his gang, who are waiting for him at the station, alone. So Kane writes his will before going out to meet Miller and his gang as the clock strikes high noon.

Truly one of the great westerns of all time, Gary Cooper has never been better. You realize that he is truly afraid of dying, but he realizes that he cannot compromise his self respect for his survival. Indeed, he understands that he must face the gang, not for the townspeople but for himself.

A truly outstanding cast, in addition to Cooper and Kelly, includes Lloyd Bridges, Thomas Mitchell, Lon Chaney, Jr., Harry Morgan, and Katy Jurado as a former girlfriend of Kane who obviously still has feelings for him.

So who wins out, The Frank Miller gang of four, or Gary Cooper? Do you have to ask? After all, this is Gary Cooper.

High Noon won four Oscars, including Best Actor for Gary Cooper, Best Film Editing, Best Musical Score, and Best Song ("Do Not Forsake Me, Oh My Darlin"), sung by Tex Ritter several times throughout the film. Losing out to *The Greatest Show on Earth* for Best Picture was one of the biggest upsets in Oscar history, and a terrible decision, I might add.

> Two of the members of Frank Miller's gang were future star Lee Van Cleef, and recording artist Sheb Wooley, whose biggest hit was the 1958 novelty hit, "The Purple People Eater." The third was Robert Wilke, who was also in *The Magnificent Seven* and got knifed by James Coburn.

Gary Cooper, getting ready to meet four bad guys alone – so he thinks! - in *High Noon*

2. *The Westerner* - 1940

Cole Harden (Gary Cooper) just doesn't look like a horse thief, Jane-Ellen Matthews tells Judge Roy Bean (Walter Brennan in an Oscar-winning performance) as she steps up to the bar. Cole says he can't take them with him, so he empties all of his coins on the bar to buy drinks for the jury. He notices two big pictures of actress/singer Lily Langtry behind the bar. Cole says he has met the Jersey Lily, whom the hanging judge adores; he even has a lock of her hair.

Hanging is delayed for two weeks, giving Cole time to get in the middle of a range war between cattlemen and homesteaders and to still be around when legendary international star Lily Langtry, former mistress of Edward VII, arrives in Texas for a performance. Harden agrees to take Bean to see the great Miss Langtry, where additional problems ensue.

While Gary Cooper is listed as the "Westerner" and star of this film, the movie clearly belongs to Brennan as the key central figure. Somehow this ruthless hangman judge without a shred of humanity winds up as at least a somewhat sympathetic figure, clearly because of Brennan's performance.

The film's cast includes Doris Davenport as Jane-Ellen, Forrest Tucker, Chill Wills, and an early appearance by future star Dana

Andrews as one of the homesteaders. Brennan won his third Best Supporting Actor Oscar for this film, and he clearly deserved it.

> The real Lily Langtry (1853-1929) was celebrated as a young woman of beauty and charm, who later established a reputation as an actress and producer. Her looks and personality attracted interest, commentary, and invitations from artists and society hostesses. She was also known for her relationships with noblemen, including the Prince of Wales, the Earl of Shrewsbury, and Prince Louis of Battenberg. But not for Judge Roy Bean, I guess.

Walter Brennan and Gary Cooper in *The Westerner*. Coop is trying to delay his hanging by providing details of his relationship with actress Lily Langtry.

3. Sergeant York – 1941

Sergeant York tells the true story of the most decorated American soldier of World War I. Alvin York (Gary Cooper), a poor young Tennessee hillbilly, is an exceptional marksman, but a country hick prone to drinking and fighting, which does not make things any easier for his patient mother (Margaret Wycherly). He changes when he meets Gracie Williams (Joan Leslie), and works night and day to buy a good farm so she'll marry him. One night he is struck by lightning during a rainstorm. Finding himself outside the meeting house where a revival is going on, he goes in and undergoes a religious awakening and vows never to lose his temper with other people again. Under the guidance of the local preacher, played by Walter Brennan, he makes amends with the men who cheated him out of the land and tries to make amends with Gracie.

When the U.S. declares war in World War I, York tries to avoid induction into the Army as a conscientious objector because of his religious beliefs, but is drafted nonetheless. His status as a conscientious objector is rejected since his local church has no official standing, and he reluctantly reports to Camp Gordon for basic training. His superiors discover that he is a terrific marksman and decide – against his wishes - to promote him to corporal.

After a sign from God which basically gives him the "render to Caesar, render to God" message, York reports back for duty and tells his superiors that he can serve his country and will leave his fate in the hands of God.

His unit is shipped out to Europe and participates in an attack during the Meuse-Argonne Offensive on October 8, 1918. Severely outnumbered but maneuvering so that the Germans believe they are surrounded, York forces a captured officer at gunpoint to order the Germans to surrender to the few Americans left alive. He and the handful of other survivors end up with 132 prisoners. York becomes a national hero and is awarded the Medal of Honor.

Arriving in New York City, York receives a ticker tape parade and a key to the city. York rejects offers to capitalize on his fame monetarily, saying that he was not proud of what he did in the war, but it had to be done. When he returns home, the people of Tennessee have purchased for him the bottomland farm he wanted and paid for a house to be built on the land.

GOOD GUYS, BAD GUYS, AND SIDEKICKS IN WESTERN MOVIES

4. *Vera Cruz* – 1954

Vera Cruz is a special favorite of mine because it stars two of my all-time favorite movie stars, Gary Cooper and Burt Lancaster.

After the American Civil War, American mercenaries travel to Mexico to fight in the Mexican revolution - for money. The former soldier and gentleman Benjamin Trane (Gary Cooper) meets the gunman and killer Joe Erin (Burt Lancaster) and his men, and together they are hired by the Emperor Maximillian and the Marquis Henri de Labordere to escort the Countess Marie Duvarre (Denise Darcel) to the harbor of Vera Cruz. Ben and Erin find that the stagecoach is transporting three million dollars in gold hidden below the seat and they scheme to steal it. Along their journey, betrayals and incidents happen changing their initial intentions.

Cooper and Lancaster make a good team with distinctive personalities. Cooper's character is pretty much the straight shooter, while Lancaster's is the schemer who is always looking for an angle to make himself rich. This buddy/conflict leads to the inevitable showdown at the end of the film.

Coop and co-star Burt Lancaster in Vera Cruz

5. *The Plainsman* – 1936

An early, classic telling of the Wild Bill Hickok/Calamity Jane/Buffalo Bill story, which certainly has some factual information but also a great deal of fiction in the storyline.

With the end of the American Civil War, and the assassination of President Lincoln, the manufacturers of repeating rifles find a profitable means of making money selling the weapons to the Great Plains' Indians, using the front man John Lattimer to sell the rifles to the Cheyenne. While traveling in a stagecoach with Calamity Jane and William "Buffalo Bill" Cody and his young wife Louisa Cody, who want to settle down in Hays City, Kansas and manage a hotel, Wild Bill Hickok finds the guide Breezy wounded by arrows and saying that the Indians are attacking a fort using repeating rifles. Hickok meets Gen. George A. Custer who assigns Buffalo Bill to guide a troop with ammunition to help the fort. Meanwhile the Cheyenne kidnap Calamity Jane, forcing Hickok to identify himself in order to rescue her.

The two leads – Gary Cooper as Hickok and Jean Arthur as Calamity Jane – have great chemistry and are on screen either individually or together about 90 percent of the time. Cooper is particularly noble as Hickok (I'm sure a lot more noble than the real Wild Bill, according to what I have read). An excellent supporting cast includes Charles Bickford as Lattimer, Gabby Hayes as Breezy, and James Ellison, surprisingly good as Buffalo Bill Cody.

> George "Gabby" Hayes played in almost 200 films thorough his career, which spanned the 1920s through the early 1950s. By the later 1930s, he worked almost exclusively as a Western sidekick to stars such as John Wayne, Roy Rogers, and Randolph Scott. He was also the inspiration for the Gabby Johnson character in the 1974 hit, *Blazing Saddles*, and that character's main line of dialogue was right out of a Gabby Hayes movie – "I wash born here, an I wash raised here, and dad gum it, I am gonna die here, an no sidewindin' bushwackin', hornswagglin' cracker croaker is gonna rouin me bishen cutter."? What did he say?

GOOD GUYS, BAD GUYS, AND SIDEKICKS IN WESTERN MOVIES

George "Gabby" Hayes. Now he REALLY looks like someone you would meet in the Old West!

One of the supporting actors in this film was a fellow named Richard Alexander. While you might not remember the name, you might recall him if I told you that he played Prince Barin in the first two *Flash Gordon* serials. He here is pictured with Buster Crabbe – Flash Gordon – and the lovely Priscilla Lawson – Princess Aura.

47

GOOD GUYS, BAD GUYS, AND SIDEKICKS IN WESTERN MOVIES

6. *Along Came Jones* - 1945

Along Came Jones is a quirky Western that stars and is also produced by Gary Cooper. Riding into Payneville, easy-going cowboy Melody Jones (Cooper) is mistaken by the townsfolk for notorious gunman Monte Jarrad (Dan Duryea) The real Jarrad is hiding out wounded on the ranch of childhood sweetheart Cherry De Longpre (Loretta Young). At first, she has the idea of sending Jones off to decoy the pursuing posse and distract the townsfolk, but once Jones has met Cherry, her feelings start to change, as do his.

I selected this Western because Gary Cooper spoofs his own slow-talking, slow to act western persona in this film. Also, as the producer, it is interesting to note that Cooper had a Western town built at the movie ranch for this film, a town which was then used in many other productions during the next 10-plus years and became a fixture in B-Westerns in particular.

If you have never seen a movie with Dan Duryea, you have really missed something. A really nice guy in real life, he almost always played sleazy scumbags in his films – often but not always westerns. (A notable exception was *Lady on a Train*, where we thought – erroneously – that he was the murderer when it was really Ralph Bellamy.)

Western villain Day Duryea – more on him later.

48

7. Friendly Persuasion – 1956

Technically not a Western – this movie takes place in Indiana during the Civil War – but it certainly has the feel of a Western.

Friendly Persuasion is the story of a family of Quakers in Southern Indiana in 1862. The Birdwell family lives an idyllic life in mid-19th century Indiana, pursuing their Quaker faith – opposing violence and war - with few challenges more upsetting than father Jess's (Gary Cooper) "unholy" purchase of a pump organ, which leads his straitlaced wife, Eliza (Dorothy McGuire), to spend a few nights sleeping in the barn.

When the Civil War moves into the state, however, it upsets their peaceful existence. Elder son Josh (Anthony Perkins in his first starring role) follows his own conscience and signs up for battle. When Josh is injured and an old family friend killed, Jess almost goes to battle himself. Even Eliza takes a broom to a hungry Confederate soldier out to make a meal of the family's pet goose. Their struggle with faith during turbulent times provides a rare insight into one of America's founding religions and makes this a monumental film.

Friendly Persuasion was nominated for six Oscars, including Best Picture, Best Director (William Wyler), and Best Soundtrack and Song. Cooper is outstanding as the patriarch attempting to balance the requirements of his religion with the reality of everyday life, and a war that tore the country apart.

Summary

While Gary Cooper excelled in a number of film genres, he really made his mark as a Western hero. Between Cooper and John Wayne, they are easily my two favorite western stars of the 30's, 40's, and 50's.

4. RANDOLPH SCOTT – 1898-1987

More than anyone else on this list, Randolph Scott was primarily a western star. In fact, it would not be an exaggeration to call Scott almost exclusively a star of westerns. While he did star in other movie genres, from the late 1940s on, in the latter part of his career, westerns were just about all that he was in.[9]

All that you need to know about the influence of Randolph Scott as a western hero can be gleaned from Mel Brooks' 1974 hit, *Blazing Saddles*. The new black sheriff is trying unsuccessfully to get the people of the small western town of Rock Ridge to allow immigrants and black people to become members of their town. He is going nowhere with his plea until he finally says, "You'd do it for Randolph Scott, wouldn't you?" The people of Rock Ridge then lift their arms

---

[9] According to my count, all 36 of his movies made between 1948 (*Albuquerque*) and his final film in 1962 (*Ride the High Country*) were, in fact, westerns.

toward heaven and sing a chorus of "Randolph Scott!" and agree to let the others join their community.

My favorite Randolph Scott westerns are:
1. Ride the High Country
2. Ride Lonesome
3. The Tall T
4. Seven Men From Now
5. Western Union
6. The Last of the Mohicans

BIOGRAPHY

Randolph Scott was a good-looking leading man who developed into one of Hollywood's greatest and most popular western stars. Born George Randolph Scott, on January 23, 1898, to George and Lucy Crane Scott, Scott was raised in Charlotte, North Carolina to a well-to-do family. He attended Georgia Institute of Technology but, after a football injury sidelined him, he transferred to the University of North Carolina and graduated with a degree in textile engineering and manufacturing (no dummy here and not typical for a future Hollywood star to have a college degree.)

> Scott served in France as an artillery advisor during World War I. His wartime training in handling and shooting weapons gave him experience that would be put to use in his film career, including how to ride a horse.

While in college, Scott discovered acting in school plays and developed a love for the theater that took him to California in 1928, with a letter of introduction from his wealthy father to no less than millionaire filmmaker Howard Hughes. Hughes got an audition for Scott for Cecil B. DeMille' *Dynamite*, a role that would go instead to Joel McCrea. Scott and McCrea would go on to become close friends and star in one film together, Scott's last film, *Ride the High Country*.

Because of his dialect and riding ability, Scott was hired to coach Gary Cooper in a Virginia dialect for *The Virginian* (1929) and also had a bit part in the film. (I guess Virginia is close enough to North Carolina to have a similar dialect.) Paramount scouts saw him in a play and offered him a movie contract.

Scott met Cary Grant, another Paramount contract player and not yet a star, on the set of a film called *Hot Saturday* (1932) and the two young actors immediately became best friends and roommates. Their on-and-off living arrangement would last until 1942, including some speculation – never proven, I might add – that they were lovers.[10] Scott married and divorced wealthy heiress Marion DuPont in the late 1930's. During this time, he moved into leading roles at Paramount with his easygoing personality.

A pleasant enough personality in comedies, dramas, and the occasional adventure film, it was not until he began focusing on westerns in the late 1940's that he reached the stardom that he was ultimately known for. His screen persona became that of a stoic, craggy, man-of-few-words type, an uncompromising figure, often a tough, hard-bitten man that was completely different from the light comedy leads he had played before that. This personality, of course, became what we think of when we envision western heroes. Scott became one of the top ten box-office stars of the 1950s (he was already in his 50's) in westerns directed by Budd Boetticher for Ranown Productions, which Scott owned.

By this time, Scott worked almost exclusively in Ranown westerns, in which he was partnered with the veteran producer Harry Joe Brown. This trio of Scott, Brown, and Boetticher produced many of the

---

[10] In a book called *Hollywood Gays* (1996) Boze Hadleigh, author of several books purporting to "out" the homosexual orientation of celebrities, makes various claims regarding Scott's homosexuality. Again, never proven.

finest medium-budgeted westerns ever made – nothing on the order of *High Noon, Shane, Red River,* or *The Searchers*, but still pretty darn good western flicks.

While Scott was still in top physical condition, his face became weary and weather beaten, which was actually perfect for the roles he was playing. This appearance, combined with his deliberate characterizations of soft-spoken, fatalistic, yet supremely reliant men, brought a new dimension of his performances that unfortunately was greatly ignored until recent years, when his films started showing up on Turner Classic Movies and Encore's Western channel, where one can regularly find a Randolph Scott flick. His final film, a less-heroic-than-usual role (rare for Scott) turned into one of his best and one of the best westerns ever made, *Ride the High Country*, in 1962. Scott retired from film making at the age of 64, right after this film was completed.

A multimillionaire as a result of many shrewd investments and reportedly worth several hundred million dollars – I said he was no dummy – Scott spent his remaining years playing golf and avoiding film industry affairs, stating that he did not like publicity. He supported both Barry Goldwater and Ronald Reagan in their presidential bids and attended the 1964 convention that nominated Goldwater for president. After a series of illnesses in his later years, Scott died in 1987 at the age of 89, survived by his second wife – of 43 years, Patricia Stillman – and his two adopted children, Christopher and Sandra. Scott is buried in his home town of Charlotte, North Carolina.

> According to the International Movie Data Base (IMDB) Scott's theory on publicity was "Never let yourself be seen in public unless they pay for it. The most glamorous, fascinating star our business ever had was Greta Garbo. Why? Because she kept herself from the public. But take the other stars of today. There is no mystery about them. The public knows what kind of toothpaste they use, whether they sleep in men's pajamas, and every intimate fact of their lives."

AWARDS AND RECOGNITION

Randolph Scott has a star on the Hollywood Walk of Fame, as do most of the others in this book. He was also nominated for a Laurel Award in 1958. Scott won a Golden Boot award in 1997 posthumously.[11]

MY FAVORITE RANDOLPH SCOTT WESTERNS

1. *Ride the High Country* - 1962

Directed by Sam Peckinpah, many fans of western movies – including me – believe that *Ride the High Country* rather than *The Wild Bunch* – is Peckinpah's finest western. The film is the story of two aging gunfighters, played by Randolph Scott and Joel McCrea at the end of their careers who try to find redemption and peace in the early 1900's, when the Old West was slowly giving way to the more modern west. Ex-marshal Steve Judd (McCrea), an honest but aging lawman, is hired by a bank to transport a gold shipment through dangerous territory to its destination.

Steve hires an old friend, former lawman and partner, Gil Westrom (Scott) and Westrom's young friend Heck Longtree to assist him. What Steve doesn't know is that Westrom plans to steal the gold, with or without the help of Steve.

On the journey to their destination, the three men get involved with a young woman's desire to escape from her father, a religious fanatic, so that she can join her fiancé. Unfortunately, her fiancé and his brothers turn out to be dangerous psychos without a shred of decency, never mind manners.

---

[11] The Golden Boot award is given to movie people – actors, directors, writers, and stunt people – who had significant involvement in the western genre in movies and television. Scott was certainly worthy of that award for his contribution to western films.

GOOD GUYS, BAD GUYS, AND SIDEKICKS IN WESTERN MOVIES

This union leads to several complications, including a shootout that pits a reunited McCrea and Scott, along with Longtree and the young woman, against the four psychotic brothers.

This movie was released in 1962 and then virtually discarded by MGM but has grown to be considered a true western classic, and rightly so. It also served as the end of the careers of both McCrea (virtually his swan song) and Scott (his actual swan song). While McCrea is his usual heroic self, Scott steals the film as the former lawman who has become an outlaw in his later years but who switches back to the side of law and order to help his friend when it counts most. The scenery is beautiful, and Scott and McCrea play off each other very well as McCrea attempts to understand why his old buddy has switched to the dark side, and Scott is torn between stealing the gold and helping his old friend.

An unusually strong supporting cast includes Mariette Hartley in her film debut as the young woman, R.G. Armstrong as her father, Ron Starr as Heck Longtree, and Edgar Buchanan – remember him from "Petticoat Junction"? as a judge. The brothers are played by James Drury (of The Virginian television show) as the fiancé, John Anderson, Warren Oates, and L.Q. Jones. This is a must see for all western fans!

The final scene – with old friends McCrea and Scott reunited against the bad guys in a shootout to the finish – is one of the best scenes in western movie history.

Joel McCrea and Randolph Scott – dynamic duo

2. *Ride Lonesome* - 1959

Ben Brigade (Randolph Scott) a bounty hunter, captures a wanted murderer, Billy John. Brigade intends to take him to the town of Santa Cruz to be hanged. He stops at a supply station, where he saves the late station manager's wife, Carrie Lane (Karen Steele) from an Indian attack, and enlists the help of two outlaws to continue the journey to safety. However, the Indian attacks persist, and the outlaws plan to take Billy John themselves as their bounty because they are tempted by the offer of amnesty for his captors – it seems they are also wanted by the authorities, and returning Billy John will get them off the proverbial hook.

At the same time, Billy's brother Frank is determined to rescue his younger brother before he can be tried for murder. But Brigade has plans of his own. It seems that Brigade and Frank have an old score to settle, and Billy is the bait. Through it all, Brigade has to make sure that no harm comes to Carrie Lane as he escorts her to safety. (He is, after all, Randolph Scott.)

Ride Lonesome is an excellent example of a Randolph Scott western directed by the venerable Budd Boetticher in which an older and wizened Scott (61 at the time) battles the elements, the bad guys, and maybe the men who are helping him as the group treks across the rugged terrain to reach the town of Santa Cruz. I like the fact that Scott is his typical man of few words but rugged action, and the viewer can't see how he is going to get out of this mess alive, with villains chasing him and potential enemies in his own ranks.

While the drop-dead gorgeous Karen Steele serves as a pleasant distraction throughout the film, the villains include James Best and Lee Van Cleef as Billy John and Frank, and the guys on Scott's side – maybe – are Pernell Roberts (before his *Bonanza* days as Adam Cartwright), and James Coburn, before his days as *Our Man Flint*.[12]

---

[12] James Coburn played a lot of villains in westerns before his breakthrough role in The Magnificent Seven in 1960.

GOOD GUYS, BAD GUYS, AND SIDEKICKS IN WESTERN MOVIES

Plus, the action sequences are impressive, and it is noteworthy to watch Scott's riding skills at the age of 61.

> Karen Steele starred in many westerns and was also the brother-in-law's wife in the film classic, *Marty*, with Ernest Borgnine as the New York City butcher. Karen grew up in Hawaii and was living in Honolulu as a young girl when Pearl Harbor was attacked on December 7, 1941. She was certainly one of the most beautiful actresses ever to work in films. I am sure that not many supply station manager's wives in the Old West really looked like Karen Steele. Western expansion might have been faster if more of them did.

Karen Steele, probably not as a supply station manager's wife.

3. *The Tall T* - 1957

The Tall T is one of Scott's most adult westerns and features a superb cast led by Randolph Scott, Maureen O'Sullivan, and Richard Boone.

Having lost his horse in a ill-advised bet, Pat Brennan (Scott) hitches a ride with a stagecoach carrying older newlyweds, Willard and Doretta Mims. Since Brennan knows the stagecoach driver (played by veteran western film actor Arthur Hunnicutt) well, he is welcome to join up and sit with him. At the next station the coach and its passengers fall into the hands of a trio of outlaws headed by a man named Usher (Richard Boone). When Usher learns that Doretta (O'Sullivan) is the daughter of a rich copper-mine owner, he decides to hold her for ransom. O'Sullivan's husband tries to use his new wife and her father's fortune as a bargaining chip to buy his way out of his predicament (but he is no match for Usher when it comes to bargaining). Tension builds over the next 24 hours as Usher awaits a response to his demands while a romantic attachment grows between Brennan and plain Jane Doretta. Brennan realizes that the outlaws are never going to let their captives get out of this predicament alive and understands that he and Doretta are going to have to outfox the bad guys to stay alive.

There is lots of brutality and tension – sexual and otherwise – for a Randolph Scott film. The lead outlaw, Usher, is not without merits of his own and yet is a vicious killer. His two very junior partners, Chink and Billy Jack, played by Henry Silva and Skip Homeier, are basically thugs who have never known anything but the life of an outlaw. There is basically no way that Brennan and Doretta can possibly get out of this mess alive, but remember, this is a Randolph Scott film.

Arthur Hunnicutt was a western character actor who often played old geezers and frontiersmen. Born in Arkansas in 1910, he did a lot of stage work in New York, Massachusetts and other places before landing in Hollywood permanently in 1949. He was a character actor in tons of westerns and was even nominated for a Best Supporting Actor role in *The Big Sky* in 1952. More about him later!

GOOD GUYS, BAD GUYS, AND SIDEKICKS IN WESTERN MOVIES

Previous page. Arthur Hunnicutt, probably as Davy Crockett. Now here's someone who actually looks like he is right out of the Old West.

4. *Seven Men From Now* – 1956

Seven Men from Now is another Scott vehicle that features Scott coming to the rescue of a attractive wife with a completely worthless husband. The film is the first of a number of Scott films directed by the outstanding director of western movies, Budd Boetticher.

This film provides a more challenging role for Scott than he normally was offered. Scott plays a morally ambiguous ex-sheriff (Ben Stride) who, while helping an Eastern husband and wife (the beautiful Gail Russell) travel cross-country in their covered wagon, hunts for the seven men who shot and killed his wife during an express office robbery. Scott has always unfairly blamed himself for his wife's murder. Along the way they are joined by two n'eer-do-wells, Masters (Lee Marvin) and Clete (Don "Red" Barry), who know that Stride is after the express-office robbers. They plan to let Stride lead them to the bandits, then make away with the loot themselves while disposing of Stride.

The scenes between Scott and Russell are strangely moving and effective, as Scott wonders why such an attractive and good woman puts up with such a worthless husband. The final showdown between Scott and Marvin (out in the middle of nowhere) is stunning.

> Gail Russell's life story was a truly tragic one. A local Hollywood high school beauty, she was signed to a contract by Paramount Studios at age 18 with virtually no acting experience of any kind. The studio gave her some alcohol to settle her nerves on the set but unfortunately, she became an alcoholic and died penniless at the age of 36 after only 28 films.
>
> Russell had a few good roles, including *The Wake of the Red Witch* and *Angel and the Badman* with her favorite leading man and true friend, John Wayne.

GOOD GUYS, BAD GUYS, AND SIDEKICKS IN WESTERN MOVIES

The beautiful Gail Russell. Maybe I am imagining it, but I detect a definite sense of sadness in her eyes.

5. *Western Union* – 1941

When Edward Creighton (Dean Jagger) leads the construction of the Western Union telegraph to unite East with West, he hires a Western reformed outlaw (Randolph Scott) and a greenhorn Eastern surveyor (Robert Young, well before his days as TV's *Marcus Welby, M.D.*) Vance Shaw (Scott) agrees to give up outlawing and go to work for the telegraph company installing poles and cables, while his brother Jack Slade leads outlaws trying to prevent the company connecting the line between Omaha and Salt Lake City.

Produced by Fox in 1941, *Western Union* was directed by Fritz Lang. This was only the second time the great German director directed a western. He had done an excellent job the year before with Fox's *The Return Of Frank James* and would have only one more western outing in 1952 with the splendid *Rancho Notorious*. Lang was no John Ford or Howard Hawks when it came to directing westerns but with *Western Union* he turned in a solid western that holds up very well today. Beautifully photographed by Edward Cronjager, it boasted a good cast that in addition to Scott, Young, and Jagger included Barton MacLane as Jack Slade. The female lead is taken by Virginia Gilmore who really has little to do in the picture..

I am not really sure why Young has top billing over Scott, since neither was a huge star at the time. It is clearly Scott's picture from the very beginning when we first see him in the film's terrific opening scene being chased by a posse across the plains. Young doesn't have much to do throughout the movie and seems out of place here.

An actor who never really distinguished himself in films, Young appeared in a string of forgettable romantic comedies in the forties and fifties culminating with his greatest success as Jim Anderson in "Father Knows Best" in the 1950's and as "Marcus Welby MD" in the seventies. And yes, that is James Brolin as his assistant, Dr. Steven Kiley. Young died in 1998 at the age of 91.

6. *The Last of the Mohicans* – 1936

The second sound version of the James Fenimore Cooper novel – the 1932 version stared Harry Carey – the 1936 film stars Scott as Hawkeye in what is probably his breakthrough film role. Overall, Scott acquits himself quite well and the movie is very watchable.

The film takes place during the French and Indian War, which preceded the Revolutionary War by about 20 years. In 1756, Fort William Henry on Lake George, New York is under siege by the French and Hurons under General Montcalm. Alice and Cora Munro, young daughters of the British Commander, Colonel Munro, set out from Albany to join their father at the fort. They are accompanied by Major Duncan Heyward, who has loved Alice for a long time, and by a renegade Huron Indian named Magua. Magua leads the party astray with the view of betraying them into the hands of a wandering party of Hurons, but his plans are foiled by Hawkeye, a British Colonial scout, when he and his comrades, Chingachgook and his son Uncas, of the Mohican tribe, rescue the party and conduct them safely to the fort.

Shortly afterwards, Munro surrenders on honorable terms to Montcalm and is permitted to march out of the fort under arms and colors. He is then mortally wounded by Magua during a massacre by the Indians as the fort is being evacuated. Cora and Alice are carried off by Magua, and Heyward, aided by Hawkeye, Chingachgook and Uncas, sets out in search of the two sisters. While Hawkeye acts nobly throughout and is the main character in the book and in the film, a fight to the finish between Chingachgook and Magua is really the climax of this western.[13]

Randolph Scott is effective as the Cooper hero, Hawkeye, is his best early screen role. The film also stars Binnie Barnes as Alice, Henry Wilcoxon as Duncan Heyward, and Bruce Cabot (Jack Driscoll from King Kong) as the evil Magua.

> Henry Wilcoxon was a busy supporting actor who played in several Cecil B. DeMille films, most notably *Cleopatra* (1934 version), *Samson and Delilah*, *Unconquered*, *The Ten Commandments*, and *The Greatest Show on Earth*. He also was an associate producer to DeMille.

Next Page. Henry Wilcoxon (upper right corner) in a scene from *Samson and Delilah*. The impressive cast included George

---

[13] I say "western" because even though it takes place in New York State, New York was really the "West" in 1756.

Sanders, the beautiful Hedy Lamarr as Delilah, a very young Angela Lansbury, and Victor Mature (kneeling) as Samson.

Summary

Randolph Scott was perhaps the ultimate western movie hero. At least Mel Brooks seemed to think so. Virtually always the good guy, and rarely a three-dimensional character (except perhaps in *Ride the High Country*), Scott hit his peak in good versus evil westerns in the 1950's, including many directed by Budd Boetticher. An easy-going guy on and off the screen.

5. HENRY FONDA – 1905-1982

Henry Fonda was one of those rare individuals who could do it all – drama, comedy, mysteries, costume dramas, war movies, playing Abraham Lincoln[14] and certainly westerns. While he generally was the hero in westerns, he could also be a very mean villain, as he was in a few films. Another Midwesterner who was often described as an everyman type of hero, Fonda certainly deserves to be placed in this book for his contribution to western films – just look at my list of favorite Henry Fonda westerns if you don't believe me. .

My favorite Henry Fonda westerns were the following:
1. My Darling Clementine
2. The Ox-Bow Incident
3. Warlock
4. Drums Along the Mohawk
5. Jesse James/The Return of Frank James
6. Fort Apache

---

[14] Henry Fonda played Lincoln in *Young Mr. Lincoln* in 1939, while Raymond Massey played Lincoln in *Abe Lincoln in Illinois* in 1940.

7. Once Upon a Time in the West[15]

BIOGRAPHY

Early Years

One of Hollywood's most respected actors, Henry Jaynes Fonda was born May 16, 1905, in Grand Island, Nebraska. After graduating from Omaha Central High School, Fonda enrolled at the University of Minnesota, where he intended to study journalism but eventually flunked out.

Back home in Nebraska, Fonda took a stab at acting, filling his time at the Omaha Community Playhouse, where he frequently shared the stage with Marlon Brando's mother. By the late 1920s, Fonda had made acting his full-time profession. He traveled to New England, where he hooked up with the University Players Guild, which cast him alongside other young actors, including James Stewart and Margaret Sullavan.

Film Stardom

Fonda's first big break came in the 1934 Broadway production *New Faces*. A year later, Fonda was out west in Hollywood, beginning what would become a nearly 50-year career in the movies. In 1935 Fonda made his screen debut in *The Farmer Takes a Wife*, which he had also starred in on Broadway. Over the next several years, Fonda's star status brightened with roles in *The Trail of the Lonesome Pine* (1936), *The Moon's Our Own* (1936), *Wings of the Morning* (1937), *You Only Live Once* (1937) and *Jezebel* (1938).

Critical praise came Fonda's way for his portrayal of Abraham Lincoln in the John Ford–directed biopic *Young Mr. Lincoln* (1939). A year later, Fonda teamed up with Ford again in the 1940 film adaption of John Steinbeck's *The Grapes of Wrath*. The film, which cast

---

[15] Actually made in 1968, but I placed it in this book anyway.

Fonda as itinerant farm worker Tom Joad, earned the actor his first Oscar nomination. Fonda was outstanding in the role.

Unflappable and adaptable to a variety of roles, Fonda became one of Hollywood's biggest stars, flexing his talent in a range of roles in movies such as *The Lady Eve* (1941), *My Darling Clementine* (1946), *Fort Apache* (1948), *Twelve Angry Men* (1957) and *Fail Safe* (1964). In all, Fonda appeared in more than 80 films during his celebrated career.

During World War II, Fonda served in the U.S. Navy and was honored with a Bronze Star and Presidential Citation Award. He was among the many Hollywood stars who left their film careers to serve in WWII. After the war, he continued to be very busy and made several outstanding films in the late 1950s in particular – *Mister Roberts* (1955), *War and Peace* (1956), a very under-rated Hitchcock film called *The Wrong Man* (1957), *12 Angry Men* (1957), and the western *Warlock* (1959). He continued in the 60's with films like *Advise and Consent* (1962), *A Big Hand for the Little Lady* (1966) and *Once Upon a Time in The West* (1968), just to name a few.

His final on-screen performance came in 1981, when he was cast opposite his daughter Jane Fonda, and Katharine Hepburn, in the family tale *On Golden Pond*. The film was a critical and commercial success and finally gave the ailing actor his first Best Actor Oscar. He was 76 at the time the award was bestowed upon him, making him the oldest actor ever to receive the award.

While he had a reputation for being somewhat cold and aloof off screen, he and best friend James Stewart often spent hours upon hours building model airplanes in one of their houses.

Final Years

In all, Fonda was married five times. He had three children: actors Jane and Peter Fonda, and a second daughter, Amy Fonda. While he and Jane were distant for many years – among other reasons, his strong patriotism versus her less-than-patriotic positions - towards the end of his life, they became very close. He is also the grandfather of actress Bridget Fonda.

At the time of his Oscar win, Fonda was too ill to attend the award ceremony. Instead, a proud Jane Fonda accepted the honor for him. "My father is so happy….Me and all the grandchildren are coming home with the Oscar."

Fonda died at his Los Angeles home on August 12, 1982.

AWARDS AND RECOGNITION

Henry Fonda was nominated for two competitive Best Actor Oscars – *The Grapes of Wrath* in 1941 and *On Golden Pond* in 1982 – and won for *On Golden Pond*. He was a co-producer of *Twelve Angry Men*, which was nominated for Best Picture in 1958. Fonda received an honorary Oscar in 1981 for being "The consummate actor, in recognition of his brilliant accomplishments and enduring contribution to the art of motion pictures."

Fonda received Golden Globe nominations for the same two films as above and again won for *On Golden Pond*. He also received the Cecil B. DeMille award at the Golden Globes in 1980. Fonda received three primetime Emmy Award nominations in his career, and also has a star on the Hollywood Walk of Fame, received a Western Heritage Award, and was nominated for three Laurel awards.

MY FAVORITE HENRY FONDA WESTERNS

1. *My Darling Clementine* – 1946

My Darling Clementine is simply one of the great westerns of all time, and does not get nearly the recognition that it deserves. A retelling of the gunfight at the OK corral story, the film stars Henry Fonda as the stoic Wyatt Earp and Victor Mature, who is outstanding – believe it or not! – as Doc Holliday.

Wyatt Earp (Fonda) and his brothers Morgan and Virgil ride into

Tombstone and leave brother James in charge of their cattle herd. On their return they find their cattle stolen and James dead. Wyatt takes on the job of town marshal, making his brothers deputies, and vows to stay in Tombstone until James' killers are found. He soon runs into the brooding, coughing, hard-drinking Doc Holliday (Mature) as well as the sullen and vicious Clanton clan. Wyatt discovers the owner of a trinket stolen from James' dead body and the stage is set for the Earp/Holliday long-awaited revenge. While Fonda is very reserved, Mature steals the show as the hard-drinking but learned ex-dentist. At one point in the movie, an actor the town has hired forgets the lines to Hamlet's soliloquy, so Holliday steps in and recites it in a beautiful piece of acting.

In case you are wondering where the title comes from, Holliday's girlfriend from the East, Clementine Carter, whom he left when he moved West a number of years previously, shows up about midway through the film to find out what has become of her fiancé. A stellar supporting case includes Linda Darnell as Doc's "friend" Chihuahua, Walter Brennan as Ike Clanton, John Ireland as Billy Clanton, Tim Holt and Ward Bond as Virgil and Morgan Earp, and Cathy Downs as the aforementioned Clementine.

One other interesting note: John Ireland played villains in both this film and the 1957 film on the same topic, *Gunfight at the OK Corral*, with Burt Lancaster and Kirk Douglas.

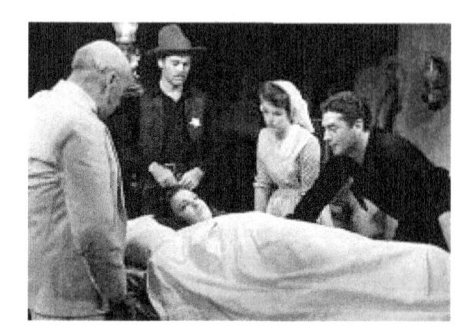

Henry Fonda, Victor Mature, and a dying Linda Darnell in *My Darling Clementine*

2. *The Ox-Bow Incident* - 1943

Speaking of great westerns that just do not get the recognition they deserve, *The Ox-Bow Incident* is perhaps number one on the list. The movie is a treatise on the dangers of vigilante justice.

Two drifters passing through a Western town (Henry Fonda and Harry Morgan) – well before his days as Colonel Potter on M*A*S*H - learn that a local rancher has been murdered and his cattle stolen. The townspeople, joined by the drifters, ignore the sage advice of the local sheriff and instead decide to form a posse to catch the murdering thieves. They find three men in possession of the cattle, and are determined to see justice done on the spot. The leader of the three men (Dana Andrews) attempts to convince the posse that he bought the cattle legally and doesn't know anything about that rancher being murdered. There are strong divisions among the members of the posse on whether to hang the three men immediately, or merely arrest them and have the local authorities deal with the issue.

Naturally, Henry Fonda, in his typical good-guy, everyman role, sides with those who recommend patience in dealing with the issue, but will they prevail? In addition to a great script, the film features an outstanding supporting cast led by Anthony Quinn as one of the suspects, Jane Darwell, William Eythe, Harry Davenport, and Marc Lawrence. It is a must-see western if you have never seen it before.

> **Dana Andrews is one of my favorite Hollywood stars of the 30s through 50s. He is most notable for playing detectives in *Laura* and *Where the Sidewalk Ends*. However, his greatest role was probably as the star of *The Best Years of Our Lives* (1946), one of the best films of the 20th century.**

3. *Warlock* – 1959

One more very under-rated western featuring a great performance by Henry Fonda as a marshal with a reputation for restoring order in troubled western towns.

The town of Warlock is plagued by a gang of thugs, leading the inhabitants to hire the formidable Clay Blaisdell (Fonda), a famous gunman, to act as marshal. Blaisdell has a reputation for coming into a town and ridding it of the undesirable characters. In fact, he tells the town leaders that they will love him at first but then want to be rid of him as soon as his mission is accomplished.

When Blaisdell appears, he is accompanied by his friend Tom Morgan (Anthony Quinn again), a club-footed gambler who is unusually protective of Blaisdell's life and reputation. At the same time, Johnny Gannon (Richard Widmark), one of the thugs who has reformed, volunteers to accept the post of official deputy sheriff as a rival to Blaisdell; and a woman (Dorothy Malone)[16] arrives in town

---

[16] Dorothy Malone was a sultry beautiful blonde leading lady of the 40s and 50s who could also really act. She won a Best Supporting Actress Oscar in 1956 for *Written on the Wind* and also starred in the television version *of Peyton Place* in the 1960s. She is still alive as of the writing of this book.

accusing Blaisdell and Morgan of having murdered her fiancé. The stage is set for a complex set of moral and personal conflicts, especially involving Fonda's character.

Fonda's character is very complex in this film: he definitely rids the town of the undesirable characters but becomes a total dictator in the process. Widmark, who starts out as an outlaw, is actually a better person than the marshal. An outstanding cast includes some memorable characters: DeForest Kelley (Bones in the original Star Trek series), Tom Drake (Judy Garland's boyfriend in *Meet Me in St. Louis*), Richard Arlen, Regis Toomey, and Wallace Ford, and Whit Bissell, who seemed to play a shopkeeper in a ton of old westerns (in addition to being the evil doctor in *I Was a Teenage Werewolf*)

Now, really! How many women in the Old West really looked like Julie Adams, Karen Steele, or Dorothy Malone.

As an example, here is a photo of Doc Holliday's real-life girlfriend, Big Nose Kate[17]. Do you see the resemblance to Dorothy Malone?

---

[17] Big Nose Kate's real name was Maria Katalin Horony. She was in Tombstone, Arizona with Doc during the famed Gunfight at the OK Corral and died in 1940 at the age of 90 in Prescott, Arizona. There is still a restaurant in downtown Prescott called Big Nose Kate's.

Big Nose Kate – you can see why

4. *Drums Along the Mohawk* – 1939

Again, essentially a western. In July 1776, Lana Borst (Claudette Colbert), the eldest daughter of a wealthy Albany, New York family, marries Gilbert Martin (Henry Fonda). Together they leave her family's luxurious home to embark on a frontier life on Gil's small farm in Deerfield, in the Mohawk Valley of central New York. However, the spirit of revolution is in the air. The valley's settlers, including Gil have formed a local militia in anticipation of an imminent war.

As Gil and his neighbors are clearing his land for farming, Blue Back (Chief John Big Tree), a friendly Oneida man, arrives to warn them that a raiding party of Seneca led by a Tory named Caldwell (John Carradine) is in the valley. The settlers evacuate their farms and take refuge in nearby Fort Schuyler. Lana, who is pregnant, miscarries during the frantic ride to the fort. The Martin farm is destroyed by the Seneca raiding party. With no home and winter approaching, the Martins accept work on the farm of a wealthy widow, Mrs. McKlennar (Edna May Oliver).

A series of skirmishes take place over the next year or so. Then during the following spring, the British and their Indian allies mount a major attack to take the valley, and the settlers again take refuge in the fort. Mrs. McKlennar is mortally wounded and ammunition runs short. Gil makes a heroic dash through enemy lines to secure help from nearby Fort Dayton. Reinforcements arrive just in time to beat back the attackers, who are about to overwhelm the fort. The militia pursues, harasses, and defeats the British force, scattering its surviving soldiers in the wilderness. The Mohawk Valley is saved, and Gil and Lana look forward to a happy and peaceful life in the new, independent United States of America.

A thoroughly well-done film with excellent performances by Fonda and Colbert, and as always, Edna May Oliver, a great character actress, is terrific as Mrs. McKlennar. She was nominated for her only Oscar in this film, but lost out to Hattie McDaniel from *Gone with the Wind*. Oliver was good, but not as good as McDaniel was in the best role of her career.

No great physical beauty, Edna May Oliver remains one of my all-time favorite supporting actresses. The list of movies she made *includes A Tale of Two Cities, David Copperfield, Little*

Women, and *Alice in Wonderland*. But my personal favorite was her outstanding performance as Lady Catherine de Bourgh in the 1940 version of *Pride and Prejudice* with Greer Garson and Laurence Olivier.

5. *Jesse James/The Return of Frank James* – 1939 and 1940

Fonda as Frank James was second fiddle to Tyrone Power as Jesse James in the 1939 version of the story of America's most famous western outlaw. Fonda then starred in the sequel made a year later, *The Return of Frank James*.

The original tells the highly fictionalized story of the James brothers - The railroads are squeezing farmers off their land and forcing them to take action. When a railroad agent kills their mother, Frank and Jesse James take up robbing banks and trains. While the public regards them as heroes, the railroads and their detectives are out to get them At one point, Jesse gives himself up to the authorities for a guarantee of a light sentence; but when the railroad changes its mind, Frank rescues him. When Jesse retires, his double-crossing friend Robert Ford shoots him in the back to get the reward. *Jesse James* features a supporting cast that includes Randolph Scott, Brian Donlevy, Nancy Kelly, Henry Hull, Jane Darwell, Donald Meek and John Carradine as the double-crossing Bob Ford.

The Return of Frank James, made a year later, obviously focuses on the life of Frank James after Jesse is killed. After the death of his brother, Frank has been laying low, living as a farmer with Clem, the young son of a former gang member. When he learns that the law is not going to go after the Fords, he decides to handle the matter himself and takes young Clem with him. To be inconspicuous they start telling people that Frank James is dead and that they witnessed his death.

Eleanor Stone, a young female reporter who wants to write about the James brothers, interviews Frank, and the two of them become very close. But eventually she learns who Frank is from the Pinkerton detective who is tracking Frank. The rest of the film is based on

Frank hunting down the Ford brothers, his trial, and the blossoming relationship between Frank and Eleanor.

A strong supporting cast includes Gene Tierney in her first film at age 20 as Eleanor Stone, an even younger Jackie Cooper as Clem, and Henry Hull, Donald Meek, and John Carradine repeating their roles from the original film.

> Any time anyone under the age of 40 tells me that Angelina Jolie – who is indeed very attractive – is the most beautiful movie star who ever lived, I just laugh and say, "Have you ever seen Gene Tierney?" She gets my vote as perhaps the most beautiful of all movie stars.

Gene Tierney, whose most famous film role was probably as Laura Hunt in the 1945 hit, *Laura*. Perhaps the most beautiful film star of all time, in my opinion.

6. *Fort Apache* – 1948

Another western in which Henry Fonda is less than a completely admirable character, Ft. Apache is one of the famed John Ford cavalry trilogy. [18] This film is reviewed under the John Wayne section. Suffice it to say that John Wayne is the straight shooter while Fonda is the arrogant, know-it-all commanding officer.

7. Once *Upon a Time in the West* – 1968

Even thought this film was made in the late 1960's, it is such a different character from the one that Fonda normally played that I have included it. It is another of those slow-paced Sergio Leone westerns (almost three hours long) that features a largely Italian cast with a few American stars – Henry Fonda, Charles Bronson, and Jason Robards, Jr. in the biggest parts.

This film is in essence the story of a young woman, Mrs. McBain (Claudia Cardinale), who moves from New Orleans to frontier Utah, on the very edge of the American West. She arrives to find her new husband and family slaughtered, but has no idea who killed them.

The prime suspect, coffee-lover Cheyenne (Jason Robards), befriends her and offers to go after the real killer, assassin gang leader Frank (a very slimy Henry Fonda in every sense of the word), in her honor. He is accompanied by Harmonica (Charles Bronson), a man also on a quest to get even with Frank. Fonda plays against type as a completely ruthless killer with no redeeming values.

The American cast also includes Woody Strode and Jack Elam as two of his henchman, and Keenan Wynn as the local sheriff and auctioneer. A must-see film if you have never seen Henry Fonda as a villain.

---

[18] *She Wore a Yellow Ribbon* and *Rio Grande* were the other two. All three films were made between 1948 and 1950, and all three movies starred John Wayne as the hero.

Summary

While everyman Henry Fonda certainly made a number of quality films in all sorts of movie genres, he was certainly no slouch when it came to quality westerns. I have mentioned seven of his best ones.

6. GLENN FORD – 1916-2006

Glenn Ford was another one of those stars like Henry Fonda in playing a wide variety of roles. While he starred in lots of westerns, he was also known for dramas, film noir, comedies, and other film genres. Like Fonda, he was generally the good guy but was also the villain in a couple of his best westerns, notably, *3:10 to Yuma* and *The Man from Colorado*.

After the war he jump-started his career with *Gilda* (1946). His career during the 1940s and 1950s showed that his talents were extensive, playing film noir in *The Big Heat* (1953), westerns like *3:10 to Yuma* (1957) and comedies like *The Gazebo* (1959) or *The Teahouse of the August Moon* (1956). He has generally been cast as a calm and collected everyday-hero, showing courage under pressure as a teacher in *Blackboard Jungle* (1955).

Ford was also no slouch when it came to real-life conflicts. He was a lieutenant colonel in the army and served in World War II, Korea, and was a consultant in Vietnam. A life-long conservative, he was among the most well liked personalities in Hollywood.

My favorite Glenn Ford westerns are the following:
1. 3:10 to Yuma
2. The Violent Men
3. Jubal
4. The Sheepman
5. The Man from the Alamo
6. The Man from Colorado
7. Cowboy

Biography

The son of a Canadian railroad executive, Gwylln Samuel Newton Ford was born in 1916 in Quebec and died at the age of 90 in 2006. His family moved to Santa Monica, California when Glenn was eight years old. Glenn's acting career began very traditionally with plays at high school, followed by acting in West Coast stage companies and a traveling theater company. In 1939 he was discovered by talent scout Tom Moore and took a screen test for Columbia Pictures, which won him a contract, although he debuted not at Columbia but in 20th-Century-Fox's *Heaven with a Barbed Wire Fence* (1939).

Columbia's boss, Harry Cohn, had spent decades observing other studios' - most notably Warner Brothers troubles with their contract stars and had built his poverty-row studio around their loan-outs. Basically, major studios would use Columbia as a "penalty box" for unruly behavior, usually salary demands or refusals to work on a certain picture. The cunning Cohn generally assigned these stars (his little studio could not normally afford then) into his pictures, and the studio's status rose immensely as the 1930s progressed. Understandably, Cohn had long resisted developing his own stable of contract stars (he'd first hired German Peter Lorre in 1934 but didn't know what to do with him) but had relented in the late 1930s, first adding Rosalind Russell, then signing Ford and fellow newcomer William Holden. Cohn reasoned that the two prospects were young unknowns with similar acting styles and could be used interchangeably, should one become troublesome.

Although often competing for the same parts, Ford and Holden became good friends. Their careers would roughly parallel each other through the 1940s, until Holden became a superstar through his remarkable association with director Billy Wilder in the 1950s. Ford made his official debut in the aforementioned *Heaven with a Barbed Wire Fence* and continued working in various small roles throughout the 1940s until his movie career was interrupted to join the Marines in World War II. Ford continued his military career in the Naval Reserve well into the Vietnam War, achieving the rank of colonel.

> With his service in three wars involving the United States, I believe Glenn Ford served in more wars than any other actor. Quite a tribute.

In 1943 Ford married legendary tap dancer Eleanor Powell, and had one son, Peter Ford. Like many actors returning to Hollywood after the war (including James Stewart and Holden) he found it initially difficult to regain his career momentum. He was able to resume his movie career with the help of Bette Davis, who gave him his first postwar break in the 1946 movie *A Stolen Life* (1946). However, it was not until his acclaimed performance in a 1946 classic film noir, *Gilda* (1946), with Rita Hayworth, that he became a major star and one of the most popular actors of his time. He scored big with the film noir classics *The Big Heat* (1953) and *Blackboard Jungle* (1955).

Ford continued to make many notable films during his prestigious 50-year movie career, but he is best known for his fine westerns such as *3:10 to Yuma* (1957) and *The Violent Men* (1954). Ford pulled a hugely entertaining turn in *The Sheepman* (1958) and starred in many more fine films. In the 1970s, Ford made his television debut in the controversial *The Brotherhood of the Bell* (1970) and appeared in two fondly remembered television series: *Cade's County* (1971) and *The Family Holvak* (1975).

During the 1980s and 1990s, Ford limited his appearance to documentaries and occasional films, including a nice cameo as Pa Kent in *Superman* (1978). He died in 2006 at the age of 90, the only one of these stars to survive into the 21st century.

AWARDS AND RECOGNITION

Glenn Ford won a Golden Globe award for Best Actor (musical/comedy) for his performance in *Pocketful of Miracles* in 1962. He was nominated for Golden Globes for Best Actor in two other films – *Teahouse of the August Moon* in 1957 and *Don't Go Near the Water* in 1958, but did not win.

He was nominated for several Laurel awards and won for Top Male Comedy Performance of 1958 for *Don't Go Near the Water*.

> The Laurel Award is given to those who, through their efforts, advance the art of film. It has nothing to do with Laurel and Hardy, although I am sure they would have been very deserving recipients.

Ford also won Golden Globe awards for most cooperative actor twice – in 1948 and 1956. He won the prestigious Golden Boot award in 1987; the Golden Boot Award honors those who have contributed specifically to western films.

Finally, Ford was reputed to be the fastest draw of any of the Hollywood male western stars of that era. Take that, John Wayne!

MY FAVORITE GLENN FORD WESTERNS

1. *3:10 To Yuma* - **1957**

This is the original, and, if I might add, superior version of the film

GOOD GUYS, BAD GUYS, AND SIDEKICKS IN WESTERN MOVIES

based on the Elmore Leonard story.

After notorious outlaw leader Ben Wade (Glenn Ford) is captured in a small town, his gang continues to threaten the locals. Small-time rancher Dan Evans (Van Heflin), whose ranch is not doing well because of drought and related conditions, is persuaded – with a large reward - to take Wade in secret to the nearest town with a railway station to await the train to the court and prison at Yuma. While Evans' wife is totally against this arrangement, fearing for her husband's safety, Evans believes he must do this for his family, even if he is killed in the process.

Of course, Wade's gang, now led by Richard Jaeckel, vows to free Ben Wade before he has to board the train. Once Wade and Evans are holed up in the hotel in town to wait the arrival of the train, it becomes apparent that getting Wade the few blocks to the train station is almost an impossible task, and a battle of wills between Wade and Evans starts.

The reason I like this version better than the 2007 version with Russell Crowe as Ben Wade is because I believe Ford's character is more complex than Crowe's. While Crowe's Ben Wade is a nasty, mean, vicious killer, Ford's Ben Wade sweet talks people into thinking that he is really a nice, down-to-earth guy behind all the criminal acts in his past. Plus, without revealing too much, I will just say that the Ford version has a happier ending than the Crowe version.

A superior cast also includes Felicia Farr in a small part as a bar maid, Leora Dana as Evans' wife, and Henry Jones as the town drunk.

Next Page. Van Heflin attempting to "escort" Glenn Ford to the train station to take Ford's character to the prison in Yuma. Heflin was a terrific actor, playing the heavy and the hero about 50 percent of the time in westerns. He won a Best Supporting Acting Oscar in 1943 for *Johnny Eager* with Robert Taylor as Eager.

GOOD GUYS, BAD GUYS, AND SIDEKICKS IN WESTERN MOVIES

2. *The Violent Men* – 1954

Imagine a solid western starring Glenn Ford, Barbara Stanwyck, Edward G. Robinson, and Brian Keith, and yet you have probably never heard of it.

The Violent Men is a 1955 CinemaScope western film drama directed by Rudolph Maté, based on the novel *Smoky Valley* by Donald Hamilton. The storyline involves a bickering married couple (Stanwyck and Robinson) at odds with cattlemen in their small town.

Parrish (Ford), a Union Army ex-officer, plans to sell his land to Anchor Ranch and move east with his fiancée, Caroline (May Wynn), but the low price offered by Anchor's "crippled" owner, Lew Wilkison (Robinson), and the outfit's bully-boy tactics make him think again. When one of Parrish's hands is murdered, he decides to stay and fight, utilizing his war experience.

Not all is well at Anchor with the owner's wife, Martha (Stanwyck), carrying on with his brother, Cole (Brian Keith), who also has a Mexican girlfriend in town. Parrish eventually gets the upper hand, and when the Wilkisons' daughter, Judith (Dianne Foster), comes to understand what her family is like and what Parrish has been up against, she realizes they can join forces as peaceful neighbors and perhaps more.

This is just a very solid, beautifully photographed western with a supporting cast that includes Warner Anderson, Richard Jaeckel (again), and Jack Kelly before he was Bart Maverick. Barbara Stanwyck and Edward G. Robinson are excellent cast choices. Apparently, Robinson was a replacement for Broderick Crawford, who fell off his horse early in shooting, and had to be replaced.[19] Personally, I like Edward G. Robinson in the part much better than Crawford.

3. *Jubal* – 1956

For a western made in 1956, Jubal has a surprisingly adult theme, and is really a terrific western. In addition to Ford, *Jubal* features a cast that includes Rod Steiger and Ernest Borgnine, both of whom were Best Actor Oscar winners during their illustrious careers.

Found injured by rancher Shep Horgan (Borgnine), Jubal Troop (Glenn Ford) is offered a job as cowhand at his ranch but soon gains Shep's trust. Mae Horgan, feeling she's been trapped into marriage with Shep, takes a definite liking to Jubal, although he is more interested in Naomi Hoktor who is travelling with a wagon train camped on Shep's land. Pinky (Steiger), until now top hand and used to Mae's favors himself, doesn't think much of the new deal and starts stirring up trouble, including false accusations against Jubal. All ends very poorly for most of the leads – except Jubal, of course. The supporting cast includes Valerie French as Mae, Felicia Farr as Naomi, Noah Berry, Jr, and a young Charles Buchinsky (we know him as Charles Bronson, of course).

> The director of this film, Delmer Daves, directed and/or wrote the screenplay for a lot of good movies, including, *3:10 To Yuma, An Affair to Remember, Broken Arrow, Pride of the Marines, Dark Passage, The Petrified Forest, The Farmer's Daughter, Destination Toyko*, and – one of my personal favorites – *Demetrius and the Gladiators*.

---

[19] International Movie Data Base (IMDB) note on this film

4. *The Sheepman* – 1958

A stranger in a Western cattle-town, Jason Sweet (Ford) behaves with remarkable self-assurance, establishing himself as a man to be reckoned with. However, Sweet soon tangles with most of the inhabitants of the town, not because of his personality but because of his livelihood. The reason appears with his stock: a herd of sheep that he won in a poker game, which he intends to graze on the cattle range. The horrified inhabitants decide to run him out at all costs. I guess the only thing worse than settlers on a cattle range was sheep on a cattle range, because the settlers at least don't eat the grass.

The first thing he does is pick a fight with the roughest, toughest man around, "Jumbo" McCall (Mickey Shaughnessy), and beat him up. He also reveals himself to be an expert with a gun. Dell Payton (Shirley MacLaine) does not know what to make of him, but is attracted to him, as is he to her. Her fiancé, local cattle baron "Colonel" Steven Bedford (Leslie Nielsen), is troubled by this and also because he and Sweet know each other. The newcomer recognizes Bedford as an old acquaintance, Johnny Bledsoe, a card sharp and gunfighter gone respectable, and decides to call in outside reinforcements. Edgar Buchanan, Pernell Roberts (before his days as Adam Cartwright on TV's Bonanza), and Pedro Gonzalez Gonzalez (no typo) round out the cast.

> If just one letter of this title had changed, the movie could have been called The Shempman instead of *The Sheepman* and could have starred Shemp Howard instead of Glenn Ford. Shemp Howard of The Three Stooges was often called The Ugliest Man in Hollywood, and you can see why. But I still loved The Three Stooges anyway. And of course, Curly Howard was my favorite Stooge.

5. *The Man from the Alamo* – 1953

Another in a long line of very good western films directed by Bud Boetticher, this time starring Glenn Ford instead of Randolph Scott.

During the war for Texas independence, one man, John Stroud (Glenn Ford) leaves the Alamo before the end (NOT a deserter but chosen by lot to ride home to help others' families protect their ranches from thieves) but is too late to accomplish his mission. He is immediately branded a coward by everyone in town.

Stroud then moves to the task of determining the gang responsible for murdering his family. And when he does realize who they are, his loss of status prevents him from exposing them. Since he cannot now expose a gang of turncoats, he infiltrates them instead. He finds out that they are out to murder the individuals heading west in a wagon train, but can he save a wagon train of refugees from this gang of Guerillas?

A top supporting cast includes Julie Adams as the female lead and wagon train member, Chill Wills as the leader of the wagon train, Victor Jory and Neville Brand as two of the evil guerillas, Hugh O'Brian (TV's Wyatt Earp), and Guy Williams (TV's Zorro.) As I always say, any wagon train with a single woman like Julie Adams on it is always worth joining up with and saving from the villains.

6. *The Man from Colorado* – 1948

A much younger and less noble Glenn Ford stars in this tale of a civil war veteran whose quest for power goes completely wrong.

Two friends, Owen Devereaux and Del Stewart (Glenn Ford and William Holden) return home after their discharge from the army after the Civil War. However, one of them (Ford) has had deep-rooted psychological damage due to his experiences during the war, and as his behavior becomes more erratic--and violent--his friend desperately tries to find a way to help him.

Because of his background in law and leadership, Devereaux is appointed as the Federal judge for the region – perhaps not the best idea for a guy with deep psychological wounds – and Stewart becomes his deputy. They both are in love with the same girl, Caroline Emmet (Ellen Drew), who marries Devereaux instead of Stewart - a big mistake, as she comes to realize.

While Stewart tries to keep Devereaux in check, Owen keeps going further and further off the deep end, which leads to the inevitable fallout and confrontation between the two men.

While Holden is fine, Ford clearly steals the show as the damaged Civil War veteran, whose idea of justice is clearly at odds with decency. A good cast includes veteran character actor Edgar Buchanan and Ray Collins as Big Ed Carter, owner of the mines and the wealthiest man in town.

> Ray Collins – Big Ed Carter – was actually only 5'8". His most famous role was, of course, as Lt. Tragg in TV's *Perry Mason* series. He was always the arresting officer, arresting the wrong suspect, of course.

Ray Collins as Inspector Tragg on "Perry Mason."

7. *Cowboy* – 1958

Another Glenn Ford western directed by Delmer Daves, this film is a fairly realistic look at what takes place on a cattle drive.

A hotel clerk in Chicago, Frank Harris (Jack Lemmon) gets jilted by his girl friend and decides to pursue his dream of becoming a real cowboy.

At the same time, Tom Reece (Glenn Ford) finishes his cattle drive and takes over an entire wing of the hotel, as usual. However, when Reece loses his profits in a poker game, Harris sees his opportunity to better himself – so he offers his entire life savings for a partnership in Reece's next drive. Reluctantly, Reece accepts.

The next morning, when Harris shows up, Reece tries to renege, not wanting to burden himself with an inexperienced greenhorn, but Harris holds him to their deal. On the cattle drive, life on the trail is not what Harris had envisioned. Reece treats him harshly, but he toughens up and Reece starts taking a liking to him. A series of adventures bringing Harris and Reese closer together is the focus for the rest of the film.

Ford is perfect as the seasoned cattle boss, a tough rancher without a lot of heart or feelings, and Lemmon is also very good as the tinhorn. The supporting cast includes Brian Donlevy, Dick York, King Donovan, and – here we go again – Richard Jaeckel.

Summary

As I have said, Glenn Ford was an actor who did well in a variety of genres – detective stories, dramas, comedies, and westerns. But he may have saved his best overall work for western films. Generally a likeable guy on and off the set and a good actor to work with.

7. RICHARD WIDMARK – 1914-2008

Richard Widmark is another one of those Western stars of this era who share similar characteristics:
  a. They were equally good at playing villains and heroes; and
  b. They made just as many non-westerns as westerns – in Widmark's case, probably even more non-westerns than westerns.

Widmark was nominated for an Oscar in his first film role – as the psycho killer Tommy Udo in the 1947 version of *Kiss of Death*, with Victor Mature starring. One of the most famous scenes in all film history is Widmark pushing wheelchair-bound Mildred Dunnock down a flight of stairs to her death.

Previous page. Mildred Dunnock, realizing that psycho killer Tommy Udo (Richard Widmark) is about to do her in, in *Kiss of Death*.

My favorite Richard Widmark westerns (a few of these spill over into the early 1960s):

1. Warlock
2. The Alamo
3. The Law and Jake Wade
4. Two Rode Together
5. Broken Lance
6. The Last Wagon
7. Yellow Sky
8. The Way West
9. Death of a Gunfighter

BIOGRAPHY

Born December 26, 1914, in Sunrise, Minnesota, Richard Widmark grew up in various locations throughout the Midwest. His father, Carl Widmark, ran a general store, and then became a traveling salesman. The family moved around a lot before settling in Princeton, Illinois, about two hours west of Chicago in the middle of farm country (which probably helps to explain his rather modest lifestyle and 55-year marriage to the same woman.)

After a turbulent childhood, brightened mainly by his frequent trips to the movies, Widmark became an accomplished high school scholar, a college football star, and eventually a teacher of speech and drama at Lake Forest College in Illinois.

Two years out of college, Widmark headed to New York City in 1938 when a friend offered him an audition for a radio soap opera. Widmark won the role, left the teaching profession, and soon became a busy worker in broadcasting and on the Broadway stage (debuting in 1943).

But despite his rising career, and happy marriage to his college sweetheart, Ora Jean Hazlewood, the 1940s were a time of great stress for the actor. Unable to serve in World War II due to a perforated eardrum, he spent three anxious years fearing for the life of his brother Donald, a bomber pilot who was injured and held as a prisoner-of-war by the Nazis.

After World War II, he was signed by 20th Century Fox to a seven-year contract. In 1947, Widmark was cast in his first film, the crime drama *Kiss of Death*, which vaulted Widmark to movie stardom. The actor made one of the most shocking film debuts in movie history as his character, the psychopath Tommy Udo, shoved an older wheelchair-bound woman down a flight of stairs to her death (while cackling with laughter, I should add.). The role earned Widmark an Oscar nomination for Best Supporting Actor and proved to be the beginning of a distinguished five-decade film career.

Stereotyped onscreen as a hot-headed villain, Widmark fought for better roles and went on to give complex performances in such film classics as *Panic in the Streets* (1950), *No Way Out* (which introduced him to close friend Sidney Poitier), *Night and the City*, *Broken Lance* (co-starring his idol, Spencer Tracy), and *Madigan*.

As the 1950s progressed, Widmark played in Westerns, military vehicles, and his old stand-by genre, the thriller. After his contract with Fox expired, Widmark formed his own production company, "Heath Productions." In 1960, he appeared in John Wayne's ode to patriotism, *The Alamo* (1960), with the personally liberal Widmark playing "Jim Bowie" in support of the very-conservative Wayne's "Davy Crockett". Not surprising because of their political differences, Wayne and Widmark did not get along particularly well. In fairness to Wayne, he was producing, directing, and starring in the film and under a lot of stress.

In 1961, Widmark acquitted himself quite well as the prosecutor in producer-director Stanley Kramer's *Judgment at Nuremberg* (1961), appearing with the Oscar-nominated Spencer Tracy and the Oscar-winning Maximilian Schell, as well as with Burt Lancaster,

Montgomery Clift, and the legendary Judy Garland (the latter two winning Oscar nods for their small roles). Despite being showcased with all this legendary acting talent, Widmark's character proved to be the foundation on which the drama turned. After all, he was the one presenting the damaging evidence against the Nazis on trial.

Widmark continued to co-star in A-pictures through the 1960s. He capped off the decade with one of his finest performances, as the amoral police detective in Don Siegel's gritty cop melodrama *Madigan* (1968). In the 1970s, he continued to make his mark in movies and, beginning in 1971, in television. In movies, he appeared primarily in supporting roles, albeit in highly billed fashion, in such films as Sidney Lumet's *Murder on the Orient Express* (1974 – he was the murder victim), Robert Aldrich's *Twilight's Last Gleaming* (1977), and Stanley Kramer's *The Domino Killings* (1977). He even came back as a heavy, playing the villainous doctor in *Coma* (1978).

In 1971, in search of better roles, he turned to television, starring as the President of the United States in the TV movie *Vanished* (1971). His performance in the role brought Widmark an Emmy nomination. He resurrected the character of "Madigan" for NBC, in six 90-minute episodes that appeared as part of the rotation of "NBC Wednesday Mystery Movie" for the Fall 1972 season.

Widmark was married for 55 years to playwright Jean Hazlewood, from 1942 until her death in 1997. He lived quietly and avoided the press, saying in 1971, "I think a performer should do his work and then shut up." *Los Angeles Times* critic Kevin Thomas thought that Widmark should have won an Oscar nomination for his turn in *When the Legends Die* (1972), playing a former rodeo star tutoring Frederic Forrest.

Widmark and Hazlewood had a daughter, Anne Heath Widmark, who was married to Hall of Fame baseball pitcher *Sandy Koufax* from 1969 to 1982). Hazlewood died in March 1997. In September 1999, Widmark married Susan Blanchard, who was Henry Fonda's third wife.

Widmark died March 24, 2008, at his home in Roxbury, Connecticut, after a long illness.

AWARDS AND RECOGNITION

As mentioned, Richard Widmark was nominated for an Oscar for his first film – *Kiss of Death* – in 1948. He won a Golden Globe Award for the same film.[20]

Widmark was nominated for a primetime Emmy for his performance in the 1971 film *Vanished*. He was also awarded a Western Heritage Award, along with John Wayne and Laurence Harvey – for *The Alamo*.

Finally, he received a career achievement award in 2005 from the Los Angeles Film Critics Association.

MY FAVORITE RICHARD WIDMARK WESTERNS

1. *Warlock* – 1959

This film has already been discussed under the films of Henry Fonda. I will merely add that Richard Widmark starts the film as a minor bad guy (member of Tom Drake's gang of ruffians who occasionally ride into town to cause trouble) and winds up being the focal point of the film. He respects Blaisdell (Fonda) but realizes the town needs a more permanent solution, since Blaisdell has become part of the problem rather than part of the solution.

This was a great western and a very good role for Widmark.

2. *The Alamo* – 1960

Directed by John Wayne and starring Wayne, Laurence Harvey and

---

[20] The Star of Kiss of Death, Victor Mature, was normally a rather wooden actor. But he was very good in this film.

Widmark, this was a pretty good version of the fight for Texas independence that was certainly plagued with too much moralizing. In 1836 General Santa Anna and the Mexican army moves across Texas in an effort to secure that area of the region for Mexico. To be able to stop him, General Sam Houston needs time to get his main force into shape.

To buy that time he orders Colonel William Travis (Harvey) to defend a small mission on the Mexicans' route north at all costs. Travis' small troop is swelled by groups accompanying Jim Bowie (Widmark) and Davy Crockett (Wayne); but as the situation becomes ever more desperate, Travis makes it clear there will be no shame if they leave while they can. Of course, we all know how that plays out – no one leaves except for Frankie Avalon (and Glenn Ford in another version of the same storyline – *The Man from the Alamo*.)

Although Wayne and Widmark did not get along at all because of their huge political differences, the film was reasonably well acted and featured lots of good battle sequences. And, as I have said, the real Davy Crockett looked more like Arthur Hunnicutt than John Wayne. But that's Hollywood for you!

A good supporting cast includes Linda Crystal, Joan O'Brien, Chill Wills, and the aforementioned Frankie Avalon, without his beach blanket attire.

> Davy Crockett was actually a Congressman from Tennessee from 1827-1831. He disagreed with President Jackson's policies on having Native Americans removed from their reservations. He wanted them to remain on their land – more progressive than Jackson, who was pretty much anti-Native American.

Crockett as a Congressman. Does not look like a backwoodsman here at all – very presentable!

3. *The Law and Jake Wade* – 1958

With Robert Taylor as the star, it is pretty obvious that Richard Widmark will be the heel in this movie, and he was. As the film opens, Jake Wade (Robert Taylor) sneaks into a jail and holds up the Marshal to spring Clint Hollister (Richard Widmark) who has been imprisoned for robbery and murder. As a result, Jake has ostensibly paid back an old debt owed his former partner from the days when the two rode together as outlaw members of Quantrill's Raiders; this included robbing banks and trains for their own personal profit even after the Civil War ended.

Jake has since completely washed his hands of his former career and has put his abilities to good use by becoming a marshal, but is satisfying his own personal code of honor by taking care of this one last debt before he marries his fiancée – Peggy - and settles down. Clint still holds a grudge for Jake's running out on him on their last bank robbery with $20,000 from that heist, from which Jake carries guilt for believing (incorrectly, as it turns out) that he had shot and killed a young boy during the robbery. That's why Jake dropped out of the gang.

Clint gathers together a gang and kidnaps Jake and Peggy, coercing Jake into taking them to the place where Jake has hidden the money. During the trip the group fights it out between themselves and with the Comanche Indians before the inevitable duel between good and evil takes place.

The Law and Jake Wade is an excellent western that demonstrates an older, wizened, battle-weary Robert Taylor – now in his late 40's – pitted against the younger Widmark, playing one of his typical sadistic (western or not!!) bad guys. Taylor's character certainly has his baggage from his outlaw days as a member of Quantrill's Raiders, but is nowhere near the nasty dude that Widmark is – a career villain. There is constant tension between the two leads throughout the film. The supporting cast includes Ray Middleton, Henry Silva, Patricia Owens, and DeForrest Kelley before his part as Bones in "Star Trek."

Adversaries Robert Taylor (in black) and Richard Widmark in The Law and Jake Wade. Taylor actually made a decent number of westerns in his time as a leading man.

4. *Two Rode Together* - 1961

This film is a bit unusual because James Stewart plays a less-than-heroic character while Richard Widmark is the straight-shooting Army officer.

In the 1880s, Marshal Guthrie McCabe (James Stewart) is content to be the business and personal partner of attractive saloon owner Belle

Aragon (Annelle Hayes), receiving ten percent of the profits. When relatives of Comanche captives demand that Army Major Fraser (John McIntire) free them, he uses a combination of army pressure and high pay to get the reluctant McCabe to take on the job of ransoming any he can find. He assigns Lieutenant Jim Gary (Richard Widmark) to accompany McCabe, and the two of them ride together – hence, the title.

Marty Purcell (Shirley Jones) is haunted by the memory of her younger brother Steve, who was abducted by the Comanches as a child. She keeps a music box that belonged to him before he was taken. McCabe warns her that Steve will not remember her because he was a young boy when he was taken years ago.

McCabe bargains with Chief Quanah Parker (Henry Brandon) and finds four white captives. Two refuse to go back, but two agree to. One is a young man named Running Wolf, who McCabe hopes is the lost son of the wealthy family. The other is a Mexican woman, Elena de la Madriaga (Linda Cristal). However, she is the wife of Stone Calf (Woody Strode), a militant rival of Parker. As they leave the camp, Stone Calf tries to take back Madriaga and is killed by McCabe, much to Quanah Parker's satisfaction.

Meanwhile, Elena finds herself ostracized by white society as a woman who degraded herself by submitting to a savage rather than killing herself. She decides to try her luck in California. Meanwhile, McCabe discovers that Belle took his deputy as a lover in his absence and got him elected to replace McCabe as marshal, causing him to complain, "I didn't get a chance to vote for myself - not even once." (He must be from Chicago.) However, he has fallen in love with Elena, so he decides to go to California with her.

The film was directed by John Ford, who could be very difficult to work with, and apparently was during this film. Both Stewart and Widmark were hard of hearing, which caused Ford to remark that he was working with two deaf guys. Additional cast members included Andy Devine, Ken Curtis, and Harry Carey, Jr.

GOOD GUYS, BAD GUYS, AND SIDEKICKS IN WESTERN MOVIES

Henry Brandon, as in *The Searchers*, plays the Indian chief, quite an accomplishment for the actor from Berlin, German, whose real name was Heinrich von Kleinbach. Not too many Native Americans were named Heinrich, I am guessing.

5.   *Broken Lance* - 1954

Once again, Richard Widmark plays a less-than-honorable character in a cast headed by Spencer Tracy as the patriarch of the cattle ranch in this CinemaScope production..

Matt Devereaux (Spencer Tracy) is a ranch owner with four grown sons. He has tried to raise them to carry on the stern, hard-working Irish settlement spirit that helped make him a success. However, as a consequence, he never learned to show his three sons from his first marriage the affection they yearned for and treats his boys little better than the hired help.

Joe (Robert Wagner) is Matt's son by his second wife, a Native American woman with the title of "Señora" (Katy Jurado). The town's people call her Señora out of respect for Matt but not out of respect for her. Because of Joe's mixed ethnicity, he is treated prejudicially by his three half-brothers, Ben (Richard Widmark), Mike (Hugh O'Brian, before his days as TV's Wyatt Earp), and Denny (Earl Holliman)—all Caucasian sons of Matt's deceased first wife.

Soon after 40 head of Matt's cattle die, Matt discovers a copper mine 20 miles away is polluting a stream where he waters his cattle. He becomes furious and leads a raid on the mine. Although the mine is on Matt's land, he does not have the mineral rights. The law issues a warrant to arrest whoever was responsible for the attack. To spare his father the agony and humiliation of being in jail, Joe claims responsibility and is sentenced to three years in prison.

With Joe out of the way, Ben and his other brothers rebel against their father with such force that the old man suffers a fatal stroke. Joe is permitted to leave prison long enough to attend his father's funeral, during which he formally severs his ties with his brothers and proclaims a blood feud. After Joe is released from prison three years later, he and Ben clash and are pitted against each other in the inevitable fight to the finish.

Hugh O'Brian was basically a supporting actor, not really a leading man, until he got the role of his life as TV's Wyatt Earp. He played that part from 1955 to 1961. Born in 1925, O'Brian died in September of 2016.

Hugh O'Brian as TV's Wyatt Earp

6. *The Last Wagon* - 1956

Sheriff Bull Harper (George Mathews) is taking "Comanche" Todd (Richard Widmark), a white man who has lived most of his life among the Indians, to be tried for the murder of Harper's three brothers. The pair join a wagon train led by Colonel Normand (Douglas Kennedy). Harper's brutal treatment of Todd causes friction with some members of the wagon train. When the sheriff beats a man for giving Todd a pipe to smoke, Todd takes advantage of the distraction to kill his tormentor.

Then, while some of the young people sneak away for a late night swim, the Apaches kill everyone else. Todd miraculously survives a fall when the wagon to which he is tied is thrown off a cliff. The Apaches are gathering to avenge the massacre of their own women and children by the whites. It is up to Todd to lead the six other survivors to safety, despite the distrust of some of them. Along the way, he and Jenny (Felicia Farr) fall in love.

Widmark plays a complex character in this under-appreciated western. The rest of the cast includes Susan Kohner, Tommy Rettig, and Nick Adams. Tommy Rettig was best known for his role as Jeff Miller on "Lassie" on television between 1954 and 1957 and was also the young boy in *The River of No Return* with Marilyn Monroe and Robert Mitchum.

7. *Yellow Sky* – 1948

"Yellow Sky" refers to the name of the ghost town that is the primary location of this film. This 1948 unheralded gem features Gregory Peck, Anne Baxter, and Richard Widmark; and when the two male leads are Peck and Widmark, you can guess who is going to be the hero and who will be the villain.

A gang of seven is on the run from the U.S. Army after robbing a bank in the Southwest. The only way out is through a salt desert (the film's location is actually Death Valley). The leader – Stretch - (Peck) decides he is following that route, while the contrarian – Dude - (Widmark) thinks it is a bad idea, but reluctantly follows the plan. After several days in the parched salt desert and nearing death from dehydration, they come across a ghost town populated only by a young but tough-as-nails girl (Baxter) and her grandfather. She shows them the location of the spring but tells them to stay away from her and her grandpa.

After a while, the gang realizes that the old man is a prospector who likely has a stash of gold stored away somewhere in town, and they decide to find it and take the gold. Trouble begins when the Peck falls for the girl and starts to identify with the girl and the old man rather than his gang. This sets up the predictable conflict between Peck and the sinister Widmark (with the rest of the gang taking sides.)

Lots of action and intrigue in this beautiful black and white western, with a good cast featuring Harry Morgan, John Russell, and James Barton as grandpa. This was Richard Widmark's fourth film, and he accounts himself favorably.

Now tell me again, how many old West women really looked like Anne Baxter? Of course, how many men looked like Gregory Peck? That's Hollywood for you!

8. *The Way West* – 1967

Featuring beautiful scenery and a trio of top-notch stars – Kirk Douglas, Robert Mitchum, and Richard Widmark – this should have been a great western. Instead, it is merely a good western that should have been even better.

In the mid-19th century, former Illinois Senator William J. Tadlock leads a group of settlers West in a quest to start a new settlement in Klamath Falls, Oregon. Tadlock (Douglas) is a highly principled and demanding taskmaster who is as hard on himself as he is on those who have joined his wagon train. He clashes with one of the new settlers, Lije Evans (Widmark) who doesn't quite appreciate Tadlock's leadership style. The guide (Mitchum) provides his skills in finding the best routes but does not really take a stand for or against Tadlock. Along the way, the families must face death and heartbreak throughout their long journey and a sampling of frontier justice meted out when one of them accidentally kills a young Indian boy.

Again, *The Way West* is a good western that should have been great. Lots of exciting adventures take place throughout the film, but the movie comes across like more of a documentary than a film. A good supporting cast includes Lola Albright, Jack Elam, Stubby Kaye, Harry Carey, Jr., and a 20-year-old Sally Field.

9. *Death of a Gunfighter* - 1969

Death of a Gunfighter is an extremely under-rated western that has Widmark playing a marshal who the townspeople eventually want to get rid of because of his overbearing approach. In the turn-of-the century Texas town of Cottownwood Springs, marshal Frank Patch is an old-style lawman in a town determined to become modern – that means more modern law enforcement. When he kills drunken Luke Mills in self-defense, the town leaders decide it's time for a change. They ask for Patch's resignation, but he refuses on the basis that the town on hiring him had promised him the job for as long as he wanted it. Afraid for the town's future and even more afraid of the fact that Marshal Patch knows all the town's dark secrets, the city fathers decide that old-style violence is the only way to rid themselves of the unwanted lawman.

Perhaps film critic Roger Ebert put it best about this film[21]: "*Death of a Gunfighter* is quite an extraordinary western. It's one of those rare attempts (the last was *Will Penny*) to populate the West with real people living in real historical time. Most Westerns could take place anywhere, anytime, if the clichés hold out."

The Marshal's fiancé was black, and there actually are Italians and Greeks in the town, but no Whit Bissell as the storekeeper. The supporting cast includes Lena Horne as his fiancé, plus Carroll O'Connor before "All in the Family," John Saxon, Dub Taylor, Larry

---

[21] May 12, 1969, *Chicago Sun Times*

Gates, David Opatoshu, and Kent Smith. It was directed by Allen Smithee, which was an alias for Don Siegel, who directed the original *Invasion of the Body Snatchers*, plus *Dirty Harry*, *Madigan*, and several other outstanding films.

I could swear that supporting actor Whit Bissell played a storekeeper in virtually every western made in the 50's. His most famous role, however, was probably the doctor in the 1957 horror classic, *I was a Teenage Werewolf,* with Michael Landon playing the lead.

Summary

Richard Widmark was an extremely versatile actor who was equally capable in westerns, crime dramas, and film noir. Perhaps more than any other western star, he was equally adept at playing heroes as well as heels. In real life, however, about as nice a guy as you would find, and never any hint of scandal.

8. GREGORY PECK – 1916-2003

We tend to think of Gregory Peck as a romantic lead in films like *Roman Holiday*, *Gentleman's Agreement*, and *The Man in the Gray Flannel Suit*; an action hero in movies like *The Guns of Navarone* and *Twelve O'Clock High*; and of course, his signature, Oscar-winning role as Atticus Finch in *To Kill a Mockingbird*. But he also starred in a number of really good western films in the 40's, 50's, and 60's. His incredibly handsome looks made him the hero in most of them, but he also took a turn or two as the villain with equal success.

My favorite Gregory Peck westerns are the following:
1. The Gunfighter
2. The Big Country
3. Yellow Sky
4. The Bravados
5. Duel in the Sun

BIOGRAPHY

Eldred Gregory Peck was born on April 5, 1916 in La Jolla, California, the son of Bernice Mary (Ayres) and Gregory Pearl Peck, a chemist and druggist in San Diego. He had Irish, English, and some German ancestry. His parents divorced when he was five years old. An only child, Peck was sent to live with his grandmother. Perhaps as a result, he had a rather lonely childhood. His fondest memories are of his grandmother taking him to the movies every week and of his dog, who followed him everywhere. When his grandmother died at age ten, his father resumed taking care of his son.

A good student, he studied pre-med at UC-Berkeley and, while there, got bitten by the acting bug and decided to change from pre-med. He was on the top-ranked Berkeley rowing team[22] and graduated with a degree in English. Peck then dropped the "Eldred" and enrolled in the Neighborhood Playhouse in New York and debuted on Broadway a short time later. His debut was in Emlyn Williams' play "The Morning Star" (1942). Exempt from military service because of a back problem, by 1943 he was in Hollywood, where he debuted in the RKO film *Days of Glory* (1944).

Stardom came with his next film, *The Keys of the Kingdom* (1944), for which he was nominated for an Academy Award. Peck's screen presence displayed the qualities for which he became well known – tall (6 foot 3), handsome, rugged, and heroic, with a basic decency that carried through most of his roles. He appeared in Alfred Hitchcock's *Spellbound* (1945) as an amnesia victim accused of murder. In *The Yearling* (1946), he was again nominated for an Academy Award and won the Golden Globe. He was especially effective in westerns and appeared in such varied ones as David O.

---

[22] Peck was mentioned in *The Boys in the Boat*, the story of the University of Washington rowing team that won the 1936 Olympic rowing championship. UC-Berkeley was Washington's primary rival in the college ranks.

Selznick's poorly reviewed *Duel in the Sun* (1946), the somewhat better received *Yellow Sky* (1948) and the acclaimed *The Gunfighter* (1950). He was nominated again for the Academy Award for his roles in *Gentleman's Agreement* (1947), which dealt with anti-Semitism, and *Twelve O'Clock High* (1949), a story of high-level stress in an Air Force bomber unit in World War II.

With a string of hits to his credit, Peck made the decision to only work in films that interested him. He continued to appear as the heroic, larger-than-life figures in such films as *Captain Horatio Hornblower R.N.* (1951) and *Moby Dick* (1956). He worked with Audrey Hepburn in her debut film, *Roman Holiday* (1953). Peck finally won the Oscar, after four nominations, for his performance as lawyer Atticus Finch in *To Kill a Mockingbird* (1962), the role for which he will be remembered forever. In the early 1960s he appeared in two darker films than he usually made, *Cape Fear* (1962) and *Captain Newman, M.D.* (1963). He also gave a powerful performance as Capt. Keith Mallory in *The Guns of Navarone* (1961), an action picture that was one of the biggest box-office hits of that year and featured a cast that included David Niven and Anthony Quinn.

In the early 1970s Gregory Peck produced two films, *The Trial of the Catonsville Nine* (1972) and *The Dove* (1974), when his film career stalled. He made a comeback playing, somewhat woodenly, Robert Thorn in the horror film *The Omen* (1976). After that, he returned to the bigger-than-life roles he was best known for, such as *MacArthur* (1977) and the monstrous Nazi Dr. Josef Mengele in the huge hit *The Boys from Brazil* (1978). In the 1980s he moved into television with the mini-series *The Blue and the Gray* (1982) and *The Scarlet and the Black* (1983). In 1991 he appeared in the remake of his 1962 film, playing a different part, in Martin Scorsese's *Cape Fear* (1991). He was also cast as the progressive-thinking owner of a wire and cable business in *Other People's Money* (1991).

Peck was awarded the U.S. Presidential Medal of Freedom. Always politically progressive, Peck was active in such causes as anti-war protests, workers' rights and civil rights. He died in June 2003, aged 87. Peck was married twice and had five children; his second marriage lasted almost 50 years.

I remember watching him on one television special where he talked about his relationship with his close friend and conservative Republican Charlton Heston. He commented that he could not figure out why Heston was so pro gun rights, but that Heston probably could not understand some of his views either.

AWARDS AND RECOGNITION

Gregory Peck was a highly recognized and awarded actor. He was nominated for five competitive Best Actor Oscars for the following films:
- *The Keys of the Kingdom* – 1944
- *The Yearling* – 1946
- *Gentleman's Agreement* – 1947
- *Twelve O'Clock High* – 1949
- *To Kill a Mockingbird* – 1962 – won the Oscar

Peck was nominated for eight competitive Golden Globes and won five of them, including Best Actor for *Captain Newman, M.D.* and Best Actor for *To Kill a Mockingbird*. Because of his charitable efforts and recognition as a good guy, he received the Jean Hersholt Humanitarian Award at the 1968 Academy Awards, and the Cecil B. DeMille Award at the 1969 Golden Globes.

He received many other awards throughout his long career.

MY FAVORITE GREGORY PECK WESTERNS

1. *The Gunfighter* – 1950

Reformed Gunfighter Jimmy Ringo (Gregory Peck) is on his way to a quiet western town in the hope of a reunion with his estranged sweetheart and their young son whom he has never seen. On arrival, a chance meeting with some old friends including the town's Marshal gives the repentant Jimmy some hope that he can put aside his reputation and start a new life.

But as always Jimmy's reputation has already caught up with him, this time in the form of three vengeful cowboys hot on his trail and a local gunslinger hoping to use Jimmy to make a name for himself. With a showdown looming, the town is soon in a frenzy as news of Jimmy's arrival spreads. His movements are restricted to the saloon while a secret meeting with his son can be arranged, giving him hope for a long term reunion with his family far removed from his wild past.

There is a certain sadness and a sense of quiet desperation in Peck's character that makes this an extremely good Gregory Peck film. For example, there is a scene where a local tough kid wants to know how he can be the next Jimmy Ringo. Peck's reply is that no matter how tough and fast you think you are, there will always be someone who is faster. A good supporting cast includes Helen Westcott, Millard Mitchell, Jean Parker, Karl Malden, Richard Jaeckel, and Skip Homeier as the tough kid who thinks he can outdraw Jimmy Ringo.

Millard Mitchell was a solid supporting actor, a sidekick in many famous westerns and non-westerns. In addition to his performance in *The Gunfighter*, he also appeared in *Winchester '73*, *Twelve O'Clock High*, and *Singin' in the Rain*.

2. *The Big Country* – 1958

The *Big Country* is a big budget, almost three hour long western with a host of stars, with Gregory Peck as the headline performer. Sprawling is the best way to describe this western.

Retired and wealthy New England sea Captain James McKay (Peck) arrives in the vast expanse of the West to marry fiancée Pat Terrill (Carroll Baker). McKay is a man whose values and approach to life are a mystery to the ranchers – it seems he thinks that people should try to get along and not kill one another over land. As a result, Terrill ranch foreman Steve Leech (Charlton Heston) takes an immediate dislike to him.

Jim soon comes to realize that Pat is spoiled, selfish and controlled by her wealthy father, Major Henry Terrill (Charles Bickford), not exactly the kind of wife he was expecting. The Major is involved in a ruthless war over watering rights for cattle, with a roughneck clan led by Rufus Hannassey (Burl Ives).

The land in question is owned by Julie Maragon (Jean Simmons), also an old friend – and former sweetheart - of Jim, and both Terrill and Hannassey want her land. Hannassey would love to have his brutal, violent older son Buck (Chuck Connors) marry her as a way of getting that property. The climax of the film is a fight to the finish between Terrill and Hannassey.

Directed by William Wyler with a superior cast, *The Big Country* is a breathtaking western. Burl Ives won a Best Supporting Actor Oscar for his performance, and Chuck Connors is also particularly good as his son. Peck holds his own as the central figure in this excellent western.

> We tend to think of Burl Ives as a singer/song writer ("Have a Holly Jolly Christmas") but he was a good actor also when given the chance.

Easterner Peck being driven to his new home by Charlton Heston in The Big Country.

3. *Yellow Sky* – 1948

I have already covered this film under the films of Richard Widmark. Let me add that Peck is clearly the lead in this film. He makes a complete turnabout from being the leader of the group of bandits to identifying with the young girl and her grandfather.

4. *The Bravados* – 1958

The Bravados is a very interesting 1958 western with revenge as its major theme.

Jim Douglas (Gregory Peck) is a rancher pursuing four outlaws after the brutal rape and murder of his wife six months before. He rides into Rio Arriba, where four men, Alfonso Parral (Lee Van Cleef), Bill Zachary (Stephen Boyd), Ed Taylor (Albert Salmi) and Lujan (Henry Silva), are in jail awaiting execution. After seeing the men in their jail cells, Douglas decides to stay and watch the execution. While there, he meets Josefa Velarde (Joan Collins) whom he met five years previously in New Orleans. She has been looking after her late father's ranch. Douglas reveals he has a daughter (Maria Garcia Fletcher). While Jim waits to witness their execution, they escape with the help of their supposed hangman; and the townspeople enlist Douglas' aid to hunt down and recapture or kill them. The rest of the film deals with his pursuit of the supposed killers, one at a time, with a rather surprising twist near the end of the film.

The hangman in the film is played by none other than Joe DeRita. He is best known for playing Curly Joe in The Three Stooges feature films of the 1960's. He was the last of the Stooges to pass away.

The Stooge on the left is Curly Joe DeRita.

Another typically beautiful movie western woman – Joan Collins

5. *Duel in the Sun* – 1946

Duel in the Sun was Gregory Peck's sixth film and first western. It was another bigger than life production, directed by King Vidor. It somewhat missed the mark but was still a worthwhile performance by Peck.

When her father is hanged for shooting his wife and her lover, half-breed Pearl Chavez (Jennifer Jones) goes to live with distant relatives in Texas. Welcomed by Laura Belle (Lillian Gish) and her elder lawyer son Jesse (Joseph Cotten), she meets with hostility from the ranch-owner himself, wheelchair-bound Senator Jackson McCanles (Lionel Barrymore), and with lustful interest from womanizing, unruly younger son Lewt (Gregory Peck as essentially the villain). Almost at once, the already-existing family tensions, including those between the two brothers, are exacerbated by her presence and the way she is physically drawn to Lewt.

With a cast like this – also including Charles Bickford, Walter Huston, Herbert Marshall, and Harry Carey – the film should have been a masterpiece but somewhat misses the mark. Most reviewers said there was too much emphasis on love and lust and not enough focus on story and character. But Peck and Jennifer Jones – too beautiful people – make a good duo.

A young Gregory Peck and Joseph Cotten in *Duel in the Sun*. You can tell that Peck has something nasty in mind.

Summary

Gregory Peck was an outstanding actor, as evidenced by his five Oscar and eight Golden Globe nominations. He was extremely versatile as an actor in action pics, dramas, and comedies, and he also made his fair share of quality westerns. Perhaps the best single word to describe him – on and off screen – is stalwart.

9. Burt Lancaster – 1913-1994

Granted, Burt Lancaster was not primarily a western star, but he made a number of really good westerns during his long career in Hollywood. He was handsome, a really good actor with a powerful presence – he was extremely athletic[23], having started his career as a

---

[23] For an example of his athleticism, just watch *The Crimson Pirate*. He was incredible, along with his pal, former circus performer Nick Cravat.

trapeze artist – and the camera was extremely friendly to him. Along with John Wayne, he is my favorite male movie star of that era, so I definitely had to include him in my book.

My favorite Burt Lancaster westerns of that era were the following:

1. Gunfight at the OK Corral
2. Vera Cruz
3. The Unforgiven
4. The Kentuckian
5. The Rainmaker
6. The Professionals
7. Apache

BIOGRAPHY

Burton Stephen Lancaster was born on November 2, 1913, in New York City and raised in East Harlem. After a stint at New York University, which he attended on an athletic scholarship, he quit to join the circus, where he worked as an acrobat and trapeze artist because of his superior athletic ability. An injury forced Lancaster to give up the circus in 1939, and he worked a series of jobs until he was drafted into the Army in 1942.

Three years later, while on leave, Lancaster's acting career was launched after he went to visit the woman who would become his second wife at the theatrical office where she was employed; there, he was asked by a producer's assistant to audition for a Broadway play. He got the part, as an Army sergeant – good casting, I guess - and soon got noticed by Hollywood. In 1946, Lancaster made his film debut opposite Ava Gardner in *The Killers,* based on an Ernest Hemingway short story. Lancaster stars as The Swede, a former boxer who gets mixed up with the mob and waits to be murdered by hit men. This was a great first film for an actor, and Burt was terrific in his debut film.

He went on to star in the 1951 biopic *Jim Thorpe: All-American,* about the Native American Olympian – again, perfect casting if you assume you can't find a good Native American actor to play the part, and 1952's *The Crimson Pirate*, in which he put his acrobatic skills to use as the swashbuckling title character – a really good action/adventure movie. In 1953, he co-starred with Deborah Kerr and Frank Sinatra in *From Here to Eternity*, a World War II film set in Hawaii just before the attack on Pearl Harbor. The film, which contained the now-iconic scene in which Lancaster and Kerr are locked in a beachside embrace as waves roll over them, earned Lancaster his first Best Actor Oscar nomination. Among Lancaster's other movie credits during the 1950s were *Apache* (1954), in which he again plays a Native American warrior; *Sweet Smell of Success* (1957), in which he plays a ruthless gossip columnist patterned after Walter Winchell; and *Gunfight at the O.K. Corral* (1957), in which he portrays Wyatt Earp to Kirk Douglas's Doc Holliday.

During the 1960s and 1970s, Lancaster started appearing in more mature, less heroic roles. He appeared in movies such as 1960's *Elmer Gantry*, which earned him his only Best Actor Oscar for his performance as a slick con man turned preacher; 1961's *Judgment at Nuremberg*, about the World War II Nazi war-crime trials; 1962's *Birdman of Alcatraz*, which was based on the true story of a convicted murderer who becomes a bird expert while behind bars and garnered Lancaster another Best Actor Oscar nomination; Italian director Luchino Visconti's 1963 historical drama *The Leopard*, in which Lancaster plays an aging aristocrat; 1968's *The Swimmer*, based on a John Cheever story; the 1970 disaster movie *Airport*; and 1979's *Zulu Dawn*, with Peter O'Toole and Bob Hoskins.

In 1980, Lancaster co-starred in director Louis Malle's *Atlantic City* and his performance as an aging gangster earned him his fourth Best Actor Academy Award nomination. He was also featured in *Local Hero* (1983), in which he plays an eccentric oil company owner; and 1989's *Field of Dreams*, starring Kevin Costner, playing the part of Doc (Moonlight) Graham, a real Minnesota doctor who appeared in one major league baseball game.

Lancaster formed a production company with his agent, Harold Hecht, in the 1950s, and was one of the first actors in Hollywood to do so. Among his producing credits were 1955's *Marty*, which won Academy Awards for Best Picture, Best Director, Best Screenplay and Best Actor (Ernest Borgnine).

In the early 1980's he began having heart problems and suffered a series of heart attacks and strokes over the next ten years, limiting his on-screen presence to only a few roles. He died on October 21, 1994 of a heart attack in his Century City condominium.

Notified of Lancaster's death, his pal, Kirk Douglas, said their 50-year relationship had been precious. "Burt was not just an actor," Douglas added. "He was a curious intellectual with an abiding love of opera who was constantly in search of unique characters to portray. . . . Elmer Gantry . . . the Birdman of Alcatraz."

A great American movie star, and he made a few really good westerns in this era.

AWARDS AND RECOGNITION

An outstanding actor, Burt Lancaster was nominated for four best actor Oscars and won one. These include:

- *From Here to Eternity* – 1953
- *Elmer Gantry* – 1960 – won the Oscar
- *Birdman of Alcatraz* – 1962
- *Atlantic City* – 1980

He was also nominated for five Golden Globe Award and won one, again for *Elmer Gantry* in 1960.

Lancaster was also nominated for numerous other awards and won several of them, including a lifetime achievement award from the Screen Actors' Guild in 1992.

MY FAVORITE BURT LANCASTER WESTERNS

1. *Gunfight at the O.K. Corral* – 1957

Perhaps the quintessential Burt Lancaster western, with Burt as the stalwart and straight-shooting Wyatt Earp, and good buddy Kirk Douglas as the alcoholic Doc Holliday. Like most versions of this theme, it is more fiction than fact in terms of what actually took place before and after the gunfight.

Wyatt Earp (Lancaster) picks up from his post in Dodge City, Kansas to join brothers Morgan, Virgil, and James in Tombstone, Arizona to fight the notorious Clanton gang, a group of cattle thieves and assorted misfits led by Ike Clanton and Johnny Ringo. He is eventually joined by his friend, former dentist and current drunkard Doc Holliday (Douglas) and his girlfriend Kate (the aforementioned Big Nose Kate), played by Jo Van Fleet.

After a series of skirmishes, culminating in the murder of brother James (Martin Milner before his Route 66 days), the inevitable shootout between the two groups takes place, with the determined Earps plus Holliday wiping out the Clantons and their fellow thugs.

Lancaster plays Earp as strong and determined, while Douglas captures all of Holliday's illnesses and neuroses with a great deal of vigor. When asked by Kate why he would risk his own life for Wyatt, he simply replies "Because he's the only friend I've ever had." A truly outstanding supporting cast includes the beautiful Rhonda Fleming as Earp's girlfriend Laura, John Ireland as Johnny Ringo, Lyle Bettger as Ike Clanton, a young Dennis Hopper as Billy Clanton, DeForest Kelley (Dr. McCoy from Star Trek) as Morgan Earp, plus Frank Faylen, Earl Holliman and Whit Bissell in supporting roles.

> The gunfight at the O.K. corral is perhaps the most famous gunfight in the history of the old West. The fight in this film lasted about 20-25 minutes; the real gunfight took place October 26, 1881 and lasted about 30 seconds.

> While living in Los Angeles in the early 1900s, Wyatt Earp became an unpaid film consultant for several silent cowboy movies. He died in 1929 at the age of 80 – not bad for a lawman in the old West.

2. *Vera Cruz* – 1954

An early Burt Lancaster western that paired him with Gary Cooper. Just after the American Civil War, American mercenaries travel to Mexico to fight in their revolution - for money. The former soldier and gentleman Benjamin Trane (Gary Cooper) meets the gunman and killer Joe Erin (Burt Lancaster) and his men, and together they are hired by the Emperor Maximillian and the Marquis Henri de Labordere to escort the Countess Marie Duvarre to the harbor of Vera Cruz. Ben and Erin learn that the stagecoach is transporting $3 million in gold hidden below the seat and they scheme to steal it. Along their journey, betrayals and incidents happen, changing their initial intentions.

Cooper and Lancaster make a winning duo, with Cooper the sturdy, righteous one and Lancaster always looking for a bit of larceny and a quick way to make a buck. We know there is going to be the inevitable confrontation in the climax of the film, and we are not disappointed. The supporting cast includes Denise Darcell as the countess (not all that appealing of a leading lady, at least in my book), Caesar Romero as Henri, George Macready as Maximillian, plus Ernest Borgnine, Jack Elam, and Henry Brandon (he certainly gets around!).

> The classic Burt Lancaster grin as well as the Lancaster teeth were never more apparent than in this movie.

GOOD GUYS, BAD GUYS, AND SIDEKICKS IN WESTERN MOVIES

Lancaster and Cooper made a good team in this film.

3. *The Unforgiven* – 1960

This film is the 1960 version starring Lancaster, Audrey Hepburn, Audie Murphy, and Lilian Gish, not to be confused with a 1992 film – *Unforgiven* - with Clint Eastwood, Gene Hackman, and Morgan Freeman.

The Unforgiven is an off-beat western centered around racial intolerance. It focuses around a Kiowa Indian claim that the Zachary daughter is one of their own, stolen in a raid when she was very young. The dispute results in other whites' turning their backs on their neighbors, the Zacharys, when the truth is revealed by the mother. Gish is the matriarch, Lancaster is the oldest child who supports his sister – Hepburn – over anything else, while Murphy plays Cash, the hotheaded brother who reacts violently to learning his "sister" is a "red-hide Indian." He leaves the family but returns to help them fight off an Indian raid during which Hepburn kills her Kiowa brother, thus choosing sides once and for all. Charles Bickford plays the leader of the neighbors who wants to give Hepburn back to the Kiowas in the hope of avoiding a conflict.

Hepburn as a Native American is a bit of a stretch visually, but she does an otherwise credible job in the role. Lancaster is the tough, do-the-right-thing-for-my-family at all costs, while Gish is good as always as the mom. At one point Hepburn fell off a stallion, which caused a three-week delay in the production.[24]

Lillian Gish was a great American film star who starred in silent films when they were in their infancy. She was the star of D.W. Griffiths' epic *Birth of a Nation*, the big budget controversial film which attempted to place the Ku Klux Klan in a positive light. Gish died in 1993 at the age of 99.

4. *The Kentuckian* – 1955

Remember that at the time this film took place – 1820's – Kentucky was actually part of the West, so I call this film a western.

A frontiersman in 1820s Kentucky – Lancaster - finds the area too civilized for his tastes (think of him as a Davy Crockett/Daniel Boone type), so he makes plans for him and his son to leave for the wild Texas country. However, he buys an indentured servant along the way, and her presence - home cooking, for example - throws a monkey wrench into his plans to get to Texas. The supporting cast includes Dianne Foster, Diana Lynn, Walter Matthau as a whip-wielding villain, John McIntyre, and John Carradine.

This is the only film that Lancaster ever completely directed, and he found it was much more difficult than he thought it would be. At one

---

[24] From *Burt Lancaster, an American Life*, by Kate Buford.

point, Matthau told him, "You don't know what the hell you're talking about, Burt." But it is still a good film with Lancaster as the rugged outdoorsman faced with the arrival of "modern" civilization, including something called a riverboat.

5. *The Rainmaker* – 1956

Less of a western than a drama, Lancaster plays a spell-binding charlatan (think Elmer Gantry) who promises to bring rain to drought-stricken Kansas in 1913.

Lizzie Curry (Katharine Hepburn) is on the verge of becoming a hopeless old maid. Her wit and intelligence and skills as a homemaker can't make up for the fact that she's just plain homely! Even the town sheriff, File (Wendell Corey), for whom she harbors a secret yen, won't take a chance --- but when the town suffers a drought and into the lives of Lizzie and her brothers and father comes one Bill Starbuck profession: Rainmaker! Suddenly the plain Lizzie has two men vying for her affections. The film is basically a lot of interesting dialog between the two stars, but does the rainmaker actually produce rain?

There was a great deal of competition and hard feelings – at first – between Hepburn and Lancaster, two big stars with even bigger egos. In fact, Hepburn berated her co-star for showing up 25 minutes late on the first day of shooting.[25] But after that, the two stars got along really well, with a great deal of cooperative spirit and enthusiasm, said producer Hal Wallis [26] Lloyd Bridges and Earl Holliman co star as Lizzie's brothers.

6. *The Professionals* – 1966

---

[25] From *Burt Lancaster, An American Life*, page 162.

[26] *Ibid, page 163.*

Yet another western with Burt Lancaster playing a strong-willed, quick-to-action leader of men. An arrogant Texas millionaire (Ralph Bellamy) hires four professional adventurers (Lancaster, Lee Marvin, Robert Ryan, and Woody Strode) to rescue his kidnapped wife (Claudia Cardinale) from a notorious Mexican bandit played by Jack Palance. While Marvin is technically the leader of the group, Lancaster, the explosives expert, certainly has the most critical role in freeing the captured wife from her brutal kidnapper.

But as the team eventually finds out, all is not as it seems. For one thing, Marvin and Lancaster both fought for Mexican Independence along with Palance. Secondly, let's just say that Cardinale is not exactly being held against her will. The effort to extract her from the bandits makes for an exciting adventure movie, and all cast members accord themselves quite well. While Lancaster and Marvin seemed to be similar personality types, they did not get along at all on this film. Lancaster was very professional and prepared, while Marvin would routinely show up drunk and unprepared for the day's shoot.[27]

With his odd looks, Jack Palance could play almost anything – Mexicans, Indians, Romans, western bad guys, and huns. But perhaps he was best at playing psycho killers. He was, of course, the villain in *Shane* and the wizened old western guy in *City Slickers* with Billy Crystal.

---

[27] *Ibid, page 242*

7. *Apache* – 1954

This was one of at least two times that Lancaster played a native American (*Jim Thorpe, All American* was the other one that I remember.) Despite looking nothing like an actual Native American – makeup helped a bit – Burt was quite effective in both movies.

In this 1954 western, based on a true story, following the surrender of Geronimo, Massai, the last Apache warrior, is captured and scheduled for transportation to a Florida reservation. Instead, he manages to escape and heads for his homeland to win back his wife and settle down to grow crops. His pursuers have other ideas though. He has several people helping him as well as several trying to capture or kill him.

Unlike most westerns with Native Americans being pursued by the white man, this film has somewhat of a positive outcome. Jean Peters – who also looked nothing like a Native American – played his wife, and the supporting cast also included John McIntyre, a young Charles Bronson, and John Dehner.

Despite looking more like an Englishman than an apache, Burt Lancaster was, as usual, very effective in *Apache*.

Summary

I could have mentioned several other non-western Burt Lancaster films that were essentially westerns – *The Devil's Disciple*, for example, is one that stands out. In addition, Lancaster continued to make westerns in the 70s and 80s, *including Lawman, Valdez Is Coming*, and *Ulzana's Raid*.

While known primarily for dramatic roles, swashbucklers, and biographies, Burt Lancaster was also quite effective in westerns. In my opinion, he is one of the biggest stars of all time as well as an outstanding actor. When he was on screen, everything seemed to naturally focus on him.

10. Barbara Stanwyck – 1907-1990

Barbara Stanwyck was an outstanding actress, maybe the best of her era after Bette Davis and Katherine Hepburn. She was not a classic beauty, but rather mixed her toughness with solid acting skills, genuine sex appeal, and an ability to play a wide variety of roles, including both good girls and bad girls. Amazingly, although she was nominated for four Academy Awards, she never won one. That was a real oversight, in my opinion!

In a career that spanned almost 60 years, Barbara Stanwyck played villains, heroines, high society women, cowgirls, newspaper reporters, call girls, and just about everything in between. She was also the star of a few westerns, which is why I placed her in this book.

Not really a beauty in the classic Hollywood sense, she made up for it by being a really good actress. Stanwyck had a definite alluring appeal that was most easily seen in her best film, *Double Indemnity*.

Barbara Stanwyck made a number of outstanding westerns. Among my own personal favorites are the following:

My favorite Barbara Stanwyck westerns were the following:

1. Annie Oakley
2. Union Pacific
3. The Great Man's Lady
4. The Violent Men
5. The Furies
6. Cattle Queen of Montana

BIOGRAPHY

Barbara Stanwyck was born Ruby Stevens on July 16, 1907, in Brooklyn, New York. She was the fifth and last child of Byron and Catherine McGee Stevens; the couple were working-class natives of Chelsea, Massachusetts and were of English and Irish extraction, respectively.

But Barbara had a very difficult and tragic childhood. When Stanwyck was four, her mother was killed when a drunken stranger pushed her off a moving streetcar. Two weeks after the funeral, her father joined a work crew digging the Panama canal and was never seen again. Barbara and her brother Byron were raised in foster homes and then later by their sister Mildred, who was five years older than Barbara.

While in foster homes, Ruby attended various public schools in Brooklyn, where she received uniformly poor grades and routinely picked fights with the other students. One can see from this early experience how she became so mentally tough as an actress – after what she went through in her childhood, making motion pictures was probably a snap to her!

In her teens, Barbara went to work at the local telephone company for $14 a week, but she had the dream of somehow entering show business. When not working at the phone company, she sought work as a dancer. Eventually her persistence paid off. At 17, Barbara was hired as a chorus girl for the sum of $40 a week, much better than the wages she was getting from the likes of Ma Bell.

In 1928 Barbara decided to move to Hollywood, where she began one of the most lucrative careers in movie history. She was an extremely versatile actress who could play virtually any kind of part. Barbara was equally at home in all genres, from melodramas, such as *Forbidden* (1932) and *Stella Dallas* (1937), to thrillers, such as *Double Indemnity* (1944), my favorite Stanwyck film, also starring Fred MacMurray (as you have never seen him before if your point of reference is "My Three Sons"). She also excelled in comedies such as *Remember the Night* (1940), *The Lady Eve* (1941), and *Christmas in Connecticut* (1945).

As I have already indicated, she appeared in several westerns, including *Union Pacific* (1939) being one of her first, and "The Big Valley" (1965) (her most memorable television role). In 1983, she played in the ABC hit mini-series "The Thorn Birds" which did much to keep her in the eye of the public.

Barbara was considered a gem to work with for her serious but easygoing attitude on the set. Unlike many stars of her era, she was not a prima donna at all. Stanwyck worked hard at being an actress, and she never allowed her star quality to go to her head.

> Barbara Stanwyck played in more different types of movies than almost any other leading lady. Hollywood finally had the good sense to award her an honorary Oscar in 1982 for "superlative creativity and unique contribution to the art of screen acting." As I have said, why they never gave her an actual competitive award is beyond me.

Stanwyck's retirement years were active, with charity work done completely out of the limelight. Her decline in health started following a robbery and beating at her Beverly Hills home in 1981, in which a cigarette case from her second husband Robert Taylor was stolen, affecting her greatly. The following year, while filming "The Thorn Birds," the inhalation of special-effects smoke on the set caused her to contract bronchitis. The illness was compounded by her cigarette habit; she had been a smoker since age nine until four years before her death. Barbara Stanwyck died in 1990.

> In 1944, when she earned $400,000, the government listed Stanwyck as the nation's highest-paid woman. I guess she was the Oprah of her day, salary-wise.

AWARDS AND RECOGNITION

Barbara Stanwyck actually received quite a bit of recognition during her career. There are certainly three factors involved here:

1) She was in the limelight for a long time in both movies and television
2) She was a really, really good actress
3) She continued acting into a time when there was more acknowledgment given to actors and actresses than merely the Oscars or Golden Globes

Her awards included the following:

- ➤ She was a four-time Oscar nominee for Best Actress: for *Stella Dallas* in 1937, *Ball of Fire* in 1941, *Double Indemnity* in 1944, and *Sorry: Wrong Number* in 1948.

> For *Double Indemnity*, she lost out at the Oscars to Ingrid Bergman in *Gaslight*, which is certainly understandable. But I personally enjoyed Barbara's performance more – I thought it was a more difficult part.

- She was awarded the American Film Institute's Lifetime Achievement Award in 1987 for her 60 years in films.
- She won Emmys for her work in "The Barbara Stanwyck Show" (1960), "The Big Valley" (1965), and "The Thorn Birds" (1983).
- She won two Golden Globe awards, including the Cecil B. DeMille award which is given for "outstanding contributions to the world of entertainment," and was nominated for three other Golden Globes for "The Big Valley."
- Barbara won the Screen Actors Guild Life Achievement Award in 1967.

MY FAVORITE BARBARA STANWYCK WESTERNS:

1. *Annie Oakley* – 1935

This is not to be confused with the 1950's musical, *Annie Get Your Gun*, with Betty Hutton and Howard Keel. In the earlier Stanwyck film, she plays the heroine with a touch of innocence and gusto. She is terrific in the title role.

In a sharpshooting match, the manager of a Cincinnati hotel bets on the fellow who's been supplying the hotel with quail...who turns out to be young Annie Oakley.[28] Result: Annie is hired for Buffalo Bill's Wild West Show (which is faithfully re-enacted in the film). She's tutored in showmanship by champ Toby Walker. But when Annie wins top billing, professional rivalry conflicts with their growing personal attachment, leading to misunderstanding and separation. After all, as Hutton said in the musical version, "You can't get a man with a gun."

A good supporting case includes Preston Foster as Toby Walker plus Melvyn Douglas, Moroni Olsen, Pert Kelton, Andy Clyde, and Chief Thunderbird as Chief Sitting Bull. By the way, that's the same Andy Clyde who played in many comedy shorts of the 1930s. And the same

---

[28] Annie Oakley's real name was Phoebe Ann Moses. Annie Oakley was her stage name, in essence.

Pert Kelton who was the original Alice Kramden on "The Honeymooners" before Audrey Meadows took over.

Barbara Stanwyck as Annie Oakley

The real Annie Oakley, sharpshooter.

2. *Union Pacific* – 1939

One of the last bills signed by President Lincoln authorizes pushing the Union Pacific Railroad across the wilderness to California. But financial opportunist Asa Barrows hopes to profit from obstructing it. Chief troubleshooter Jeff Butler (Joel McCrea) has his hands full fighting Barrows' agent, gambler Sid Campeau (Brian Donlevy); Campeau's partner Dick Allen (Robert Preston) is Jeff's Civil War friend and is also a rival suitor for engineer Monahan's daughter Molly Monahan (Barbara Stanwyck). Who will survive the effort to push the railroad through at any cost? The film also included DeMille regular Lynne Overman, a young Anthony Quinn, Evelyn Keyes, and Lon Chaney, Jr.

Produced and directed by Cecil B. DeMille, *Union Pacific* and *Stagecoach* – released at roughly the same time – were responsible for raising westerns from cheap B movies to major films.

Apparently, Robert Preston did not think much of DeMille as a director – he said DeMille only cared about action, not acting. However, that did not stop Preston from appearing in two other DeMille films in the next three years, *Northwest Mounted Police* in 1940 and the highly successful *Reap the Wild Wind* in 1942.

3. *The Great Man's Lady* – 1942

In Hoyt City, a modern metropolitan city in the West, a statue of city founder Ethan Hoyt (Joel McCrea) is being dedicated, and 100 year old Hannah Sempler Hoyt – Barbara Stanwyck – (who lives in the last residence among skyscrapers) is at last persuaded to tell her story to a "girl biographer." Flashback: to 1848, when teenage Hannah – a Philadelphia rich girl - meets and flirts with pioneer Ethan Hoyt, who is visiting her father to secure funds for an adventure to develop the West. On a sudden impulse, they elope. The film follows their struggle to start a city in the wilderness, where they are hampered by the Gold Rush, silver mines, the railroads, star-crossed love, floods, and heartbreak. In flashback, Hannah tells her story to the biographer, from age 16 to age 100. All the trials and tribulations, including whether or not she was really married to Ethan Hoyt.

How Barbara Stanwyck did not even get an Oscar nomination for this picture is beyond me. She is terrific as she ages from 16 to 100 and is completely believable at each age. She demonstrates courage, toughness, and sweetness at alternating points in the film. The point of the film is that this so-called Great Man would never have gotten anywhere without the pluck and savvy of Hannah Sempler, his first wife. Stanwyck and McCrea worked on six films together, and they apparently got along very well professionally.

4. *The Violent Men* – 1954

This film has already been profiled under the section on Glenn Ford. Suffice it to say that Barbara Stanwyck adds her usual toughness – think *Double Indemnity* – in her role as the wife of cattle baron Edward G. Robinson. This film could easily have been called The Violent People instead.

5. *The Furies* – 1950

This Stanwyck western takes place in the 1870s, in New Mexico territory, not yet a state. T.C. Jeffords (Walter Huston) is a cattle baron who built his ranch, the Furies, from scratch. He borrows from banks, pays hired hands with his own script ("T.C.'s"), and carries on low-level warfare with the Mexicans who settled the land but are now considered squatters. He has enemies, including Rip Darrow (Wendell Corey), a saloon owner whose father T.C. took land from. T.C.'s headstrong daughter, Vance (Stanwyck), has a life-long friend in one of the Mexicans, she has her heart set on Rip, and awaits dad's promise that she will run the Furies someday. Her hopes are smashed by Rip's revenge, a gold-digger who turns T.C.'s head, and T.C.'s own murderous imperialism. Is Vance to be cursed by fury and hatred?

Here we have an excellent western filled with hatred, revenge, and double crosses – what could be better? Look at the supporting cast – Judith Anderson, Albert Dekker, Gilbert Roland, Beulah Bondi,

Thomas Gomez, and John Bromfield, just to name a few. The film was directed by Anthony Mann, an outstanding director, who directed many of James Stewart's best films.

Walter Huston – father of Director John Huston – died about a year before the film was released. He was terrific, as always, in the role of the patriarch of the Furies. He was nominated for four acting Oscars and won one, in 1948, for *The Treasure of the Sierra Madre*, with Humphrey Bogart.

6. *Cattle Queen of Montana* – 1954

OK, so this is not that great a western, but it does feature a future President of the United States – Ronald Reagan, of course, in a starring role. Robert Mitchum turned down the part because he did not care for the script, so Ronald Reagan took it. But it does feature Barbara Stanwyck.

Pop Jones (Morris Ankrum) inherits a piece of family land in Montana, so he and his daughter, Sierra Nevada – I'm not kidding - decide to leave their Texas ranch and move there. As his nononsense daughter Sierra (Stanwyck) bathes in a pond along the trail, she encounters a stranger, Farrell (Ronald Reagan), a hired gunman who warns her about dangerous Indians nearby.

Farrell is on his way to work for Tom McCord, a rich rancher. Quite a bit of rustling has been going on in the Montana territory of late. McCord is in cahoots with Indians, in particular Natchakoa of the Blackfoot tribe, whose braves stampede the Jones family's cattle, knock Sierra cold, wound her cowhand Nat, and kill Pop, after which McCord steals a document from Pop's dead body that grants rights to the land.

Sierra is nursed back to health by Colorados, a young Blackfoot who attends school among the whites, to the displeasure of the tribal chief, his father. McCord offers a $2,000 bounty to Farrell if he kills Sierra, but instead Farrell comes to her rescue.

Farrell reveals that he is actually an agent for the U.S. Cavalry, investigating the rustling and killing. With the help of Sierra, he blows up a McCord wagon filled with ammunition being sold to the Indians, doing away with McCord once and for all and bringing at least temporary peace to the area.

A good supporting cast includes Gene Evans as the evil Tom McCord, Lance Fuller as Colorados, plus Anthony Caruso and Jack Elam. Plus, this film is filled with several supporting actors who made tons of movies, whose names you may not remember but whose faces you certainly will. Among them:

Morris Ankrum played in tons of westerns as well as generals in science fiction movies. He was also the judge in 22 episodes of "Perry Mason."

Myron Healey was the heel in lots of movies, especially westerns of the 1950's.

Character actor Byron Foulger was generally cast as an owlish storekeeper, mortician, professor, or bank teller, but his better parts had darker intentions. He was exceptional as weaselly, mealy-mouthed, whining henchmen who inevitably showed their yellow streak by the film's end. He also played a scientist in *Flash Gordon Conquers the Universe*, with Buster Crabbe as Flash.

And here he is. Buster Crabbe also appeared in numerous westerns in the 30's through 50's, generally in B westerns as generally, but not always, the hero. They made him dye his brown hair blond for *Flash Gordon*, which he hated.

Summary

Barbara Stanwyck's forte was not really westerns, and her most famous western was not even a film, but a television show as the matriarch in "The Big Valley". But she was as close to a female western star – of major films, at least – as I could find. And what a terrific actress she was!

Section Two – Sidekicks and Bad Guys

A. Sidekicks

	Page
1. Walter Brennan	140
2. Gabby Hayes	146
3. Andy Devine	151
4. Slim Pickens	157
5. Katy Jurado	163
6. Harry Carey	171
7. Arthur Hunnicutt	180

B. Bad Guys

1. Dan Duryea	189
2. Neville Brand	198
3. John Ireland	207
4. Jack Elam	216
5. Victor Jory	225
6. Arthur Kennedy	233
7. John Carradine	241
8. Charles Bickford	253

For every western hero, there was at least one villain and often a sidekick to the hero. These stars were often better actors than the heroes – after all, they had to get by on their acting ability much more than their good looks. But westerns of this era would never have been as good without their presence.

Several of these stars – Walter Brennan and Arthur Kennedy come in mind – were cast as both sidekicks and villains throughout their careers. Again, there were many other individuals – Ward Bond, for example, that could have been placed on this list, but these 14 men – and one woman – had a particular appeal to me.

Sidekicks

1. Walter Brennan – 1894-1974

In many ways Walter Brennan was the most successful and familiar character actor of American sound films, and the only actor to date to win three Oscars for Best Supporting Actor. I could easily have placed him in the villains category instead of this one. People may remember him mostly for TV's "The Real McCoys," but he was much more than that.

My favorite Walter Brennan westerns from that time period are:
1. The Westerner
2. Rio Bravo
3. My Darling Clementine
4. Red River
5. Bad Day at Black Rock
6. Sergeant York

BIOGRAPHY

Born Walter Andrew Brennan on July 25, 1894 in Lynn, Massachusetts, Walter had a normal upbringing and attended college in Cambridge, Massachusetts, studying engineering. While in school he became interested in acting and performed in school plays. He worked some in vaudeville and also in various jobs such as clerking in a bank and as a lumberjack. Brennan toured in small musical comedy companies before entering the military in 1917. After his war service he went to Guatemala and raised pineapples, then migrated to Los Angeles, where he speculated in real estate, made a lot of money and then lost it during the stock market crash of 1929. A few jobs as a film extra came his way beginning in 1923, then some work as a stuntman. He eventually achieved speaking roles, going from bit parts to substantial supporting parts in scores of features and short subjects between 1927 and 1938.

In 1936 his role in *Come and Get It* (1936) won him the very first Best Supporting Actor Academy Award. He would win it twice more in the decade, and be nominated for a fourth. His range was enormous. He could play sophisticated businessmen, con artists, local yokels, cowhands and military officers with apparent equal ease. An accident in 1932 cost him most of his teeth, and he most often was seen in eccentric rural parts, often playing characters much older than his actual age. His career never really declined, and in the 1950s he became an even more endearing and familiar figure in several television series, most famously "The Real McCoys" (1957). He died in 1974 of emphysema, a beloved figure in movies and TV, the target of countless comic impersonators, and one of the best and most prolific actors of his time.

Like many Hollywood stars of that era Brennan was always fiscally and ideologically conservative. He became politically active in later life when he saw many of the things he believed in being eroded by the counterculture movement. He supported George Wallace's presidential campaign in 1968 and in 1972 supported extreme right-wing Republican Representative John Schmitz as the incumbent

President Richard Nixon was viewed as too progressive by many Republicans.

Walter Brennan played a train conductor in the first Three Stooges short – *Woman Haters* – in 1934. The Stooges attempt to induct him into the Woman Haters' Club. In reality, Brennan was actually married to the same woman for 54 years.

AWARDS AND RECOGNITION

Walter Brennan is the only actor to win three Best Supporting Actor Oscars; he won for the following films:
- *Come and Get It* – 1936
- *Kentucky* – 1938
- *The Westerner* – 1940 – maybe his best performance

He was also nominated for Best Supporting Actor for *Sergeant York* in 1941 but did not win.

Brennan was nominated for one Emmy but did not win – "The Real McCoys" in 1957, where he played grandpappy Amos.

MY FAVORITE WALTER BRENNAN WESTERNS:

1. *The Westerner - 1940*

Already discussed under Gary Cooper, this was perhaps Brennan's finest performance as real life hanging judge Roy Bean. While Gary Cooper is listed as the "Westerner" and star of this film, the movie clearly belongs to Brennan as the key central figure. Somehow this ruthless hangman judge without a shred of humanity winds up as at least a somewhat sympathetic figure, clearly because of Brennan's performance.

2. *Rio Bravo* – 1959

Already discussed under the section on John Wayne, Brennan plays the crotchety, toothless old deputy to Dean Martin's sheriff in this buddy western and holds his own against some good talent. Brennan actually was toothless and wore false teeth as the result of an accident he had in the 1930's[29]. Arthur Hunnicutt played Brennan's part in what was essentially the remake of this film, *El Dorado*.

3. *My Darling Clementine* - 1946

Already discussed under the section on Henry Fonda. Brennan is the mean and nasty head of the Clanton gang, who make the mistake of taking on the Earps and Doc Holiday. Brennan is really tough until he is the last one of his clan left, then he is not so tough after all.

4. *Red River* - 1948

Already discussed under the section on John Wayne. Brennan plays Wayne's sidekick (and cook on the trail), while befriending Wayne's adopted son, played by Montgomery Clift. He is a very sympathetic character in this film in contrast with the rough edges shown by Wayne's character – pretty much a typical Walter Brennan sidekick part – giving advice whether it is wanted or not!

5. *Bad Day at Black Rock* - 1955

---

[29] According to the John Wayne biography by Scott Eyman (*John Wayne, the Life and Legend*), Brennan was paid $10,000 a week for his work on *Rio Bravo*, not a bad sum in 1959.

A really under-appreciated Western with Spencer Tracy in the starring role. From the time John J. Macreedy (Tracy) steps off the train in the tiny desert town of Black Rock, he feels a chill from the local residents. The town is only a speck on the map and few if any strangers ever come to the place, and rightly so; it's very tiny, barren, and also very unfriendly. Macreedy himself is tight-lipped about the purpose of his trip and he finds that the hotel refuses him a room, the local garage refuses to rent him a car, and the sheriff is a useless drunkard. It soon becomes obvious to Macreedy that the locals have something to hide, but when he finally tells them that he is there to speak to a Japanese-American farmer named Kamoko, he really touches a nerve so sensitive that he will spend the rest of the movie fighting for his life.

This is another sympathetic role for Brennan, who plays the town doctor and is the only character to be pulling for Macreedy for most of the film. The rest of the cast is a good one, with Robert Ryan as the town boss and principal villain of the film, Lee Marvin and Ernest Borgnine as the town tough guys, Dean Jaggar as the do-nothing sheriff, and Anne Francis as someone caught in the middle. My single favorite scene is probably the one where the one-armed Tracy beats the snot out of town bully Borgnine in front of everyone.

6. *Sergeant York* - 1941

This "western," which takes place in extremely rural Tennessee around the time of World War I, has already been discussed under the section on Gary Cooper. Brennan plays the local preacher who leads Gary Cooper away from a life of violence and turns him into a pacifist, at least until Cooper is confronted by the reality of war. He is again effective in his role. Brennan was nominated for an Oscar but did not win.

Summary

It is a testimony to the ability of Walter Brennan that he was a sidekick, or even a villain, in so many great films, including the six listed here. Of these six films, he is the sidekick in four and the villain in two – although in *The Westerner* he is actually both the villain and the sidekick.

While he made a number of non-western films that were also very good, Walter Brennan remains probably the greatest sidekick of any western supporting star of that era. One reason these movies are so good is that Walter Brennan was in them.

2. Gabby Hayes – 1885-1969

Even if you have never seen Gabby Hayes on screen, if you saw the caricature of him in Blazing Saddles – Gabby Johnson – you basically have an understanding of his on-screen persona – craggy, bearded, tough to understand, but a lovable character nonetheless. As Olson Johnson says of the Gabby character in the film, "Now who can argue with that? I think we're all indebted to Gabby Johnson for clearly stating what needed to be said. I'm particularly glad that these lovely children were here today to hear that speech. Not only was it authentic frontier gibberish, it expressed a courage little seen in this day and age." Frontier gibberish was right on the money in the case of Gabby Hayes.

Among his best remembered phrases are the following: "consarn it", "yer durn tootin,", "dadgummit," "durn persnickety female," and "young whippersnapper." Just to name a few.

BIOGRAPHY

George "Gabby" Hayes was probably the most famous of all Western-movie sidekicks of the 1930s and 1940s. He was born May 7, 1885, the third of seven children, in the Hayes Hotel (owned by his father) in the tiny hamlet of Stannards, New York in western New York state – not in Arizona as one might have expected. George was the son of hotelier and oil-production manager Clark Hayes, and grew up in Stannards.

As a young man, George Hayes worked in a circus and played semi-pro baseball while a teenager. He ran away from home at 17 in 1902, and joined a touring stock company. Gabby married Olive Ireland in 1914 and the pair became quite successful on the vaudeville circuit. Retired in his 40s, he lost much of his money in the 1929 stock market crash and like Walter Brennan was forced to return to work. Although he had made his film debut in a single appearance prior to the crash, it was not until his wife convinced him to move to California and he met producer Trem Carr that he began working steadily in motion pictures. He played scores of roles in Westerns and non-Westerns alike, finally in the mid-1930s, settling in to an almost exclusively Western career.

Gabby gained fame as Hopalong Cassidy's sidekick Windy Halliday in many films between 1936-39. Leaving the Cassidy films in a salary dispute, he was legally precluded from using the "Windy" nickname, and so took on the moniker of "Gabby", and was so billed from about 1940 on. One of the few sidekicks to land on the annual list of Top Ten Western Box office Stars, he did so repeatedly.

In his early films, he alternated between whiskered comic-relief sidekicks and clean-shaven bad guys, but by the later 1930s, he worked almost exclusively as a Western sidekick to stars such as John Wayne, Roy Rogers, and Randolph Scott. After his last film, in 1950, he starred as the host of a network television show devoted to stories of the Old West for children, The Gabby Hayes Show (1950). Offstage an elegant and well-appointed connoisseur and man-about-town the exact opposite of his western persona, in fact, Hayes devoted the final years of his life to his investments. He was married one time for 40+ years until his wife died in 1957. Gabby died of cardiovascular disease in Burbank, California, on February 9, 1969.

Hayes appeared in almost 200 films, the vast majority of them being "B" westerns. The leading men he worked with most included John Wayne, Randolph Scott, Roy Rogers, and William Boyd (Hopalong Cassidy)

A couple of Gabby Hayes quotes that I found interesting and informative:

[On John Wayne] "He's my boy. He's the best. Couldn't think more of him if he was my own son."

[on westerns] "I hate 'em. Really can't stand 'em. They always are the same. You have so few plots--the stagecoach holdup, the rustlers, the mortgage gag, the mine setting and the retired gunslinger."[30]

It is tough to select my favorite Gabby Hayes movies for several reasons. One, he played in mostly "B" movies, and two, they all tend to blend together. With that in mind, I have selected a couple that were better than most.

1. The Plainsman
2. Tall in the Saddle

MY FAVORITE GABBY HAYES WESTERNS

1. *The Plainsman* – 1936

Directed by Cecil B. DeMille, this is a story of Gary Cooper as Wild Bill Hickok and Jean Arthur as Calamity Jane. With the end of the North American Civil War and the assassination of President Abraham Lincoln, the manufacturers of repeating rifles find a profitable means of making money by selling the weapons to the

---

[30] From International Movie Data Base (IMDB), on Gabby Hayes

North American Indians, using the front man John Lattimer to sell the rifles to the Cheyenne. While traveling in a stagecoach with Calamity Jane and William "Buffalo Bill" Cody and his young wife Louisa Cody, who want to settle down in Hays City managing a hotel, Wild Bill Hickok finds the guide Breezy (Gabby Hayes) wounded by arrows and telling him that the Indians are attacking a fort using repeating rifles. Hickok meets Gen. George A. Custer, who assigns Buffalo Bill to guide a troop with ammunition to help the fort. Meanwhile the Cheyenne kidnap Calamity Jane, forcing Hickok to reveal himself to rescue her. Gabby Hayes plays Hickok's sidekick, Breezy, with James Ellison as Buffalo Bill and Charles Bickford – almost always the baddie – as Lattimer.

2. *Tall in the Saddle* – 1944

A better than average John Wayne "B" western of the early 1940's with Gabby Hayes as trustworthy sidekick Dave. When a stranger (Wayne) arrives in a western town he finds that the rancher who sent for him has been murdered. Further, most of the townsfolk seem to be at each other's throats, and the newcomer has soon run contrariwise to most of them. Ella Raines and Ward Bond co-star in this film. *Tall in the Saddle* was filmed on location at Agoura Ranch in Agoura, California; Lake Sherwood, California; RKO Encino Ranch in Encino, California; and Sedona, Arizona. Studio scenes were shot at RKO Studios in Hollywood, Los Angeles.

Summary

Gabby Hayes was the perfect definition of the western sidekick in almost 200 films made in the 1930s and 1940s, most of which were eminently forgettable. But he was popular enough to be parodied in *Blazing Saddles*, as the ultimate trustworthy buddy who babbled a lot of gibberish.

My only real problem with Gabby Hayes is that, while I saw him in a ton of movies, most of them were "B" oaters that are not really worth mentioning here in detail. But he was often paired up with Roy Rogers and Dale Evans (for 41 films), as well as John Wayne, and

Randolph Scott in some of their lesser features. So if you want a real picture of Gabby Hayes, take a look at some of those 1930's and 40's oaters. They include titles like:

- *Bar 20 Justice*
- *Jesse James at Bay*
- *Sons of the Pioneers*
- *Gunfighter*
- *Don't Fence Me In*
- *The Old Santa Fe*
- *Smokey Smith*

3. Andy Devine – 1905-1977

Andy Devine was that rare sidekick who appeared in many really good westerns – unlike Gabby Hayes – and then had an additional career in television westerns, primarily as Jingles Jones in the Wild Bill Hickok series starring Guy Madison as Hickok. He was often the reluctant sidekick, as in *Stagecoach*.

My favorite Andy Devine movie westerns are the following:
1. Stagecoach
2. The Man Who Shot Liberty Valance
3. Canyon Passage
4. Two Rode Together
5. The Adventures of Wild Bill Hickok (television show)
6. Roy Rogers films

BIOGRAPHY

Heavy-set comic character actor of American films, Andy Devine was born Andrew Vabre Devine in Flagstaff, Arizona. Raised in nearby Kingman, Arizona, the son of Irish-American hotel operator Thomas Devine and his wife Amy. Devine was a good athlete as a student and actually played semi-pro football under a phony name (Jeremiah Schwartz, often erroneously presumed to be his real name). Devine used the false name in order to remain eligible for college football. A successful football player at St. Mary & St. Benedict College, Arizona State Teacher's College, and Santa Clara University, Devine went to Hollywood with dreams of becoming an actor. After a number of small roles in silent films, he was given a good part in the talkie *The Spirit of Notre Dame* (1931) in part due to his fine record as a football player. His sound-film career seemed at risk due to his severely raspy voice, the result of a childhood injury. As a result, he became a supporting player rather than a leading man. His voice, however, soon became his trademark, and he spent the next forty-five years becoming an increasingly popular and beloved comic figure in a wide variety of films, including and perhaps especially westerns.

In the 1950s, his fame grew enormously with his co-starring role as Jingles Jones opposite Guy Madison's "Adventures of Wild Bill Hickok" (1951), on television and radio simultaneously. In 1955, before the Hickok series ended, Devine took over the hosting job on a children's show retitled "Andy's Gang" (1955), in which he gained new fans among the very young. He continued active in films until his death in 1977. He was survived by his wife and two sons.

Things to know about Andy Devine:
- The main street of Kingman, Arizona, near his birthplace of Flagstaff is named Andy Devine Boulevard.
- He was once honorary mayor of Van Nuys, California.
- Father of Tad Devine and Denny Devine, who played his sons in *Canyon Passage* (1946).
- Was mentioned in the 1974 song "Pencil Thin Mustache" by Jimmy Buffett.
- He was a licensed amateur (ham) radio operator with the call sign WB6RER. The call is now owned by an amateur radio club in Kingman, Arizona, which holds an annual event in memory of their favorite son.

- His high-pitched squeaky voice was the result of a childhood accident. While running with a stick (some accounts say a curtain rod) in his mouth, he tripped and fell, ramming the stick through the roof of his mouth. For almost a year, he was unable to speak at all. When he did get his voice back, at length, it had the wheezing, almost duo-toned quality that would ultimately make him a star. Another account of his throat injury says he was sliding down the banister in his father's hotel and somehow damaged his throat.
- John Ford picked him to play Buck, the stagecoach driver, in *Stagecoach* (1939) because he had actual experience driving a six-horse team. This was probably the turning point in his career.
- Devine made his stage debut as Captain Andy Hawks in Guy Lombardo's 1957 production of "Show Boat" at a theatre in Long Island.
- He was an avid pilot and owned a flying school that trained flyers for the government during World War II.
- Andy had a children's television show on one of the local Los Angeles television stations called "Andy and Froggy", eventually called "Andy's Gang" and televised nationally, where his sidekick was a frog puppet. You might remember the famous line that got Froggy out of his jack-in-the-box – "Plunk your magic twanger, Froggy!"
- Andy was NOT the first choice to play Jingles Jones – Burl Ives was, but he turned down the part. I can still remember Andy yelling, "Hey Wild Bill, wait for me!"

AWARDS

Andy Devine was a 1988 recipient – posthumously – of the Golden Boot Award, given for significant achievements in western films.

MY FAVORITE ANDY DEVINE WESTERNS

1. *Stagecoach* – 1939

Already covered under the John Wayne section. Andy Devine plays Buck, the stagecoach driver who is either a friend of or has a past connection to the Ringo Kid (John Wayne). Buck is one of only two people who want to return to Apache Wells – typical for a Devine character, since he always seems to be a rather timid soul in his films.

Andy Devine and George Bancroft in Stagecoach

2. *The Man Who Shot Liberty Valance* – 1962

This film was also already covered under the films of John Wayne. In this movie, Devine plays the timid sheriff who will not cope with the likes of the no-good rotten Liberty Valance, leaving it up to the likes of James Stewart and John Wayne to take care of business. In Andy's defense, everyone else in the town was afraid of Liberty Valance except Wayne.

3. *Canyon Passage* – 1946

In 1856, backwoods businessman Logan Stuart (Dana Andrews) escorts Lucy Overmire (Susan Hayward), his friend's fiancée, back home to remote Jacksonville, Oregon. In the course of the hard journey, Lucy is attracted to Logan, whose heart seems to belong to another. Once arrived in Jacksonville, a number of subplots involve villains, fair ladies, romantic triangles, gambling fever, murder, a cabin-raising, and vigilantism...culminating with an Indian uprising that threatens all the settlers. Starring Dana Andrews – one of my all-time favorite stars, Susan Hayward – another of my favorites, and Brian Donlevy, plus Patricia Roc, Ward Bond, Hoagy Carmichael, and of course Andy Devine as Ben Dance. Great cast, great story, and great outdoor photography.

Dana Andrews and Susan Hayward, two of my favorite stars. Andrews was very under-rated as an actor, because he always underplayed his roles, never overacted. He played detectives in movies like *Laura* and *Where the Sidewalk Ends* and an occasional western like this one and *The Ox Bow Incident*. But his greatest role was certainly as an returning veteran in the classic film, *The Best Years of Our Lives*.

4. *Two Rode Together* – **1961**

Excellent western already listed under the films of Richard Widmark. Andy Devine plays Sergeant Darius P. Posey in this well-done John Ford film starring James Stewart, Richard Widmark, and Shirley Jones.

5. **"The Adventures of Wild Bill Hickok" – 1951-1958 – television show**

Even though it is a TV show, I had to put it in here. This very popular television series had nothing to do with the story of the real James Butler Hickok, nicknamed Wild Bill by his contemporaries. You'd hardly know from this show that Hickok would meet an abrupt demise in Deadwood. Or that his famous tenure as Marshal of Abilene lasted slightly over a year. The series featured the handsome Guy Madison as Hickok and the 300-pound Devine as Jingles Jones. Devine's poor pinto was always lagging behind, which resulted in the series' most famous line, "Hey Wild Bill: Wait for Me!"

6. **As Constable/Sheriff Cookie Bullfincher in a bunch of Roy Rogers and Dale Evans films in the mid to late 40's.**

Devine starred with Roy Rogers and Dale Evans in a series of low-budget oaters in the late 1940's playing constable/sheriff/judge Cookie Bullfincher, including the following:

- Bells of San Angelo – 1947
- Springtime in the Sierras – 1947
- On the Old Spanish Trail – 1947
- The Gay Ranchero – 1948 – "gay" refers to happy, not sexual orientation
- Under California Stars – 1948
- Eyes of Texas – 1948
- Night Time in Nevada – 1948
- Grand Canyon Trail – 1948
- The Far Frontier - 1948

All these films were released between April 1947 and December 1948, so you know how long it took to actually make these westerns.

Summary

Andy Devine was the perfect – often timid and reluctant – sidekick who was the perfect foil for the hero on many western films of the 1930's through 1960's. His career also extended into television in series like "The Adventures of Wild Bill Hickok" and "Andy's Gang." He was well deserving of being listed in this group of supporting players.

4. Slim Pickens – 1919-1983

Slim Pickens was an updated version of Andy Devine – heavyset, often but not always a buffoon, and the sidekick in many westerns. Unlike Devine, however, he was often cast as villains rather than sidekicks. His most famous role, however, was not a western but as Major King Kong in the black comedy classic, *Dr. Strangelove*.

My favorite Slim Pickens westerns were:
1. Blazing Saddles
2. The Cowboys
3. One-Eyed Jacks
4. The Sheepman
5. Gun Brothers
6. The Last Command

BIOGRAPHY

Slim Pickens spent the early part of his career as a real cowboy and the latter part playing cowboys, and he is best remembered for a single "cowboy" image: that of bomber pilot Maj. "King" Kong waving his cowboy hat rodeo-style as he rides a nuclear bomb onto its target in the great black comedy *Dr. Strangelove or: How I Learned to Stop Worrying and Love the Bomb* (1964).

Born Louis Burton Lindley, Jr. on June 29, 1919 in Kingsburg, near Fresno in California's Central Valley, he was the son of a dairy farmer who early on became bored with dairy farming. After that, Slim spent much of his boyhood in nearby Hanford, where he began doing rodeos at the age of 12. Over the next two decades he toured the country on the rodeo circuit, becoming a highly-paid and well-respected rodeo clown, a job that entailed enormous danger.

In 1950, at the age of 31, Slim married Margaret Elizabeth Harmon and that same year he was given a role in a western, *Rocky Mountain* (1950), starring a past-his-prime Errol Flynn. He quickly found a niche in both comic and villainous roles in that genre. With his hoarse voice and pronounced western twang, he was not always easy to cast outside the genre, but when he was, as in "Dr. Strangelove," the results were often memorable. He died in 1983 after a long and courageous battle against a brain tumor. He was survived by his wife Margaret and three children.

Interestingly, Slim Pickens played the role of Buck – Andy Devine's role – in the very inferior 1966 remake of *Stagecoach*, with the less-than-great Alex Cord playing the John Wayne role of The Ringo Kid. (Some classic films just should NEVER be remade.)

AWARDS

Slim received the Golden Boot Award for excellence in western movies in 1983.

MY FAVORITE SLIM PICKENS WESTERN FILMS

1. *Blazing Saddles* – 1974

Outside the scope of this book, but I had to put it in here. The classic Mel Brooks comedy western is the Ultimate Western Spoof. The plot concerns a town (where everyone seems to be named Johnson) that is in the way of the path of the railroad. In order to grab their land, Hedley Lamarr (Harvey Korman – don't call me Hedy Lamarr!, a politically connected nasty guy), sends in his henchmen, including Slim Pickens as Taggert, who is the boss of the railroad workers, to make the town unlivable. After the sheriff is killed, the town demands a new sheriff from the Governor (Mel Brooks). Hedley convinces him to send the town the first Black sheriff (Cleavon Little) in the West. Bart is a sophisticated urbanite who will have some difficulty winning over the townspeople. But with the help of his new deputy Jim (Gene Wilder) he eventually turns the initially racist town on his side.

Slim Pickens and Harvey Korman in a rather heated discussion in *Blazing Saddles*.

2. *The Cowboys* – 1972

When his cattle drivers abandon him for the promise of more lucrative gold fields, rancher Wil Andersen (John Wayne) is forced to take on a collection of 11 young boys, ages 9-15, as his drivers in order to get his herd to market in time to avoid financial disaster. The boys learn to do a grown man's job under Andersen's watchful eye; however, neither Andersen nor the boys know that a gang of cattle thieves is stalking them. Pickens' character is the one that suggests using the young boys from a particular school as cattle drivers. The supporting cast includes Roscoe Lee Browne, Colleen Dewhurst, Robert Carradine, and Bruce Dern as the villainous Long Hair.

3. *One-Eyed Jacks* – 1961

Running from the law after a bank robbery in Mexico, Dad Longworth (Karl Malden) finds an opportunity to take the stolen gold and leave his partner Rio (Marlon Brando) to be captured. Years later, Rio escapes from the prison where he has been imprisoned, and hunts down Dad for revenge. Dad is now a respectable sheriff in California, and has been living in fear of Rio's return. Lots of altercations before the inevitable showdown between Longworth and Rio.

This is the only film directed by Marlon Brando, and it is a good one. Slim Pickens plays the sadistic deputy to Longworth and is really mean and despicable. A good cast includes Katy Jurado as Longworth's wife, Ben Johnson, Hank Worden, Elisha Cook, Jr., and Pina Pellicer.

4. *The Sheepman* – 1958

The Sheepman has already been discussed under the section on Glenn Ford. Slim Pickens plays a timid sheriff who always seems to be missing when there is trouble brewing.

5. *Gun Brothers* – 1956

A "B" movie oater that is actually better than it should have been. Chad Santee (Buster Crabbe) heads west to join his brother, Jubal (Neville Brand), who supposedly has a large cattle ranch. On the way he meets Rose Fargo (Ann Robinson) and rescues her from the unwanted advances of a gambler, "Blackjack" (James Seay). When Chad and Rose arrive they find that Jubal and his partner, Shawnee, are really rustlers and outlaws. Jubal tries to get Chad to join them but he refuses, and leaves to set up his own homestead with Rose at his side. Later, the repentant Jubal comes to join him. Shawnee, angry at what he considers a double-cross, attacks the brothers with his gang. Costars are Michael Ansara as Shawnee and Slim Pickens as Moose MacLain.

6. *The Last Command* - 1955

The Last Command is a 1955 Trucolor Western film produced and directed by Frank Lloyd about Jim Bowie and the fall of the Alamo during the Texas War of Independence in 1836. Filmed by Republic Pictures, the picture was an unusually expensive undertaking for the normally low-budget studio. Released during the Walt Disney Davy Crockett time period with Fess Parker playing Davy Crockett in the Disney TV show, the film follows Jim Bowie (Sterling Hayden), who was initially a friend to Generalissimo Antonio López de Santa Anna (J. Carrol Naish) but now sides with the Texans in their bid for independence; and his lieutenant, William Travis, played by low budget horror film star Richard Carlson.

Crockett has a lesser role and is played by veteran character actor Arthur Hunnicutt; Hunnicutt probably looked a lot more like the real Davy Crockett than either Fess Parker or John Wayne did – a lot more regarding that later when I discuss Hunnicutt. Also featured in the film are a lot of good character actors including Ernest Borgnine, Anna Maria Alberghetti, John Russell, Jim Davis, Eduard Franz, Otto Kruger, and Slim Pickens as Abe. The film was originally supposed to star John Wayne as Crockett, but he and the director had an argument and Wayne ended up making his own version of the Alamo five years later.

Summary

An excellent character actor in westerns and other films, Slim Pickens basically picked up the Andy Devine roles 15-20 years later. But his most famous role is not a western at all – but as the bomber who rode the bomb in Dr. Strangelove. Fellow actor James Earl Jones recalls, "He was Major Kong on and off the set—he didn't change a thing—his temperament, his language, his behavior."[31] That sure sounds a lot like Slim Pickens to me.

---

[31] From Wikipedia, write-up on *Dr. Strangelove*.

5. Katy Jurado (1924-2002)

The two words I think of whenever Katy Jurado comes to mind are "Mexican spitfire." But she was much more than that. An outstanding actress, she was a standard bearer for getting Latino women better parts in films. Never shy on-screen, she always seemed to be the one who "tells it like it is," or at least like she thought it was, whether you wanted to hear it or not. While she certainly was not relegated to westerns, her most famous films seem to be in this genre.

Here are my favorite Katy Jurado westerns:
1. High Noon
2. Pat Garrett & Billy the Kid
3. The Badlanders
4. Broken Lance
5. One-Eyed Jacks

Biography

Katy Jurado was born María Cristina Estela Marcela Jurado García – try saying that ten times! - into a wealthy family on January 16, 1924, in Guadalajara, Mexico. Her early years were spent amid luxury until her family's lands were confiscated by the federal government for redistribution to the landless peasantry. When movie star Emilio Fernandez discovered Katy at the age of 16 and wanted to cast her in one of his films, Jurado's grandmother objected to her wish to become a movie actress. To get around the ban, Katy slipped from the grasp of her family's control by marrying actor Víctor Velázquez.

Jurado eventually made her debut in *No matarás* (1943) during the what has been called "The Golden Age of Mexican Cinema."[32] Blessed with stunning beauty and an assertive personality (to say the least), Jurado specialized in playing determined women in a wide variety of films in Mexico and the United States.

She used what she called her "distinguished and sensuous look" to carve a niche for herself in Mexican cinema. Her rather Indian features were unusual for a film star in Mexico, which meant that she typically was cast as a dangerous seductress/man-eater, a popular type in Mexican movies..

In addition to acting, Jurado worked as a movie columnist and radio reporter to support her family. She also worked as a bullfight critic, and it was at a bullfight that Jurado was spotted by John Wayne and director Budd Boetticher. Boetticher, who was also a professional bullfighter, cast Jurado in his autobiographical film *Bullfighter and the Lady* (1951), which he shot in Mexico. She was cast despite having very limited English-language skills and had to speak her lines phonetically.

Then she made her big breakthrough in American films in the role of Gary Cooper's former mistress, saloon owner Helen Ramirez, in *High Noon* (1952). She received two Golden Globe nominations from the Hollywood Foreign Press Association for that part, for Most Promising Newcomer and Best Supporting Actress, winning the latter.

---

[32] From Katy Jurado biography on IMDB site

> Her *High Noon* performance historically proved to be an important acting watershed for Latino women in American movies. Jurado's portrayal undermined the Hollywood stereotype of the flaming, passionate Mexican "spitfire." She was perhaps the most reasonable character in that film, with the exception of Cooper.

With her superb performance in *High Noon*, Jurado proved that Latino women could be more than just sexpots in the American cinema. Jurado was blessed with extraordinary eyes, which were both beautiful and expressive, their beauty and strength never fading with age. Two years after *High Noon*, Jurado received an Academy Award nomination as Best Supporting Actress for her role as Spencer Tracy's Indian wife in Edward Dmytryk's *Broken Lance* (1954), making her the first Mexican actress thus honored.

She refused to sign a contract with a major Hollywood studio in order to be able to return to Mexico between her American roles to star in Mexican films. Jurado remained in Los Angeles for 10 years, marrying Ernest Borgnine, her co-star in *The Badlanders* (1958), in 1959. During their tempestuous relationship, Jurado and Borgnine separated and reconciled before finally separating for good in 1961. The tabloids reported that Borgnine had abused her, and their separation proved rocky as well, as they fought over alimony. Their divorce became final in 1964. Borgnine summed up his ex-wife as "beautiful, but a tiger," a term that described her on-screen persona as well (she had two children with former husband Victor Velasquez, a daughter and a son, who tragically was killed in an automobile accident in 1981.

Jurado played the wife of Marlon Brando's nemesis Dad Longworth (Karl Malden) in *One-Eyed Jacks* (1961), Brando's sole directorial effort. In her role she also was the mother of a young woman who was Brando's love interest, thus marking a career transition point as she assumed the role of a mature woman. As Jurado aged, she appeared in fewer films, but notable among them included *Arrowhead* (1953) with Charlton Heston, *Trapeze* (1956) in support of Burt Lancaster and *Man from Del Rio* (1956) with her fellow Mexican national Anthony Quinn who, unlike Jurado, had become an American citizen. She also appeared with Quinn in *Barabbas* (1962) and *The Children of Sanchez* (1978).

Katy appeared on the Western-themed American TV shows "Death Valley Days" (1952), "The Rifleman" (1958), "The Westerner" (1960) and "The Virginian" (1962). But her career in the U.S. began to wind down, and she was reduced to appearing in "B" pictures like *Smoky* (1966) with Fess Parker and the Elvis Presley movie *Stay Away, Joe* (1968). She attempted to commit suicide in 1968, and then moved back home to Mexico permanently, though she continued to appear in American films as a character actress. Her last American film appearance was in Stephen Frears' *The Hi-Lo Country* (1998), capping a half-century-long American movie career that continued due to her talent and remarkable presence, long after her extraordinary good looks had faded.

Towards the end of her life, she suffered from heart and lung ailments. Katy Jurado died on July 5, 2002, at the age of 78 at her home in Cuernavaca, Mexico. She was survived by her daughter.

Awards and Recognition

Katy Jurado was nominated for a Best Supporting Actress Oscar in 1954 for her role in *Broken Lance*. She won a Golden Globe for Best Supporting Actress in 1953 for *High Noon*, and was also nominated for a golden globe for most promising newcomer the same year.

Jurado won three Ariel awards, the Mexican equivalent of the Oscar, a Best Supporting Actress award in 1954 for *El Bruto* (1953) a Best Actress Award for *Fe, esperanza y caridad* (1974) and a Best Supporting Actress award in 1999 for *El evangelio de las Maravillas*. She also was awarded a Special Golden Ariel for Lifetime Achievement in 1997. In the United States, she was honored with a Golden Boot Award by the Motion Picture & Television Fund in 1992.

GOOD GUYS, BAD GUYS, AND SIDEKICKS IN WESTERN MOVIES

My favorite Katy Jurado films were the following:

1. *High Noon - 1952*

High Noon has already been reviewed in the section on Gary Cooper. But let's look a Katy Jurado's important contribution. Previously, Mexican and Latino women in Hollywood films were characterized by an unbridled sexuality, as exemplified by such diverse actresses as Lupe Velez, Dolores del Rio (who came to loathe Hollywood and returned to Mexico in the 1940s), and Rita Hayworth, who was born Margarita Cansino. Although Jurado's character was forced to kowtow to the stereotype in *High Noon*, delivering such lines as, "It takes more than big, broad shoulders to make a man," her great dignity in her role as a moral arbiter among the competing factions of the marshal and his fiancée, the townspeople, and the gunmen out to kill the marshal, showed that Helen Ramirez was in control and controlled by nothing, not even her former love for the marshal. Her restrained performance, delivered with a great deal of conviction, emphasized the shortcomings of the rest of the other characters, other than Cooper's marshal. Her moral integrity is the reason she, like the marshal, decides to abandon the town.

The following dialog between Amy (Grace Kelly) and Helen Ramirez (Katy Jurado) pretty much shows the character, mental toughness, and moral fiber of Jurado's character.

Amy: That man downstairs, the clerk, he said things about you and Will. I've been trying to understand why he wouldn't go with me, and now all I can think of is that it's got to be because of you...Let him go, he still has a chance. Let him go.
Helen: He isn't staying for me. I haven't spoken to him for a year - until today. I am leaving on the same train you are...What kind of woman are you? How can you leave him like this? Does the sound of guns frighten you that much?
Amy: I've heard guns. My father and my brother were killed by guns. They were on the right side but that didn't help them any when the shooting started. My brother was nineteen. I watched him die. That's when I became a Quaker. I don't care who's right or who's wrong.

There's got to be some better way for people to live. Will knows how I feel about it.
Helen: I hate this town. I always hated it - to be a Mexican woman in a town like this.
Amy: I understand.
Helen: You do? That's good. I don't understand you. No matter what you say. If Kane was my man, I'd never leave him like this. I'd get a gun. I'd fight.
Amy: Why don't you?
Helen: He is not my man. He's yours.

2. *Pat Garrett & Billy the Kid* - 1973

This 1973 American western drama film was directed by Sam Peckinpah, written by Rudy Wurlitzer, and stars James Coburn, Kris Kristofferson and Bob Dylan. The film is about an aging Pat Garrett (Coburn), hired as a lawman by a group of wealthy New Mexico cattle barons to bring down his old friend Billy the Kid (Kristofferson). Katy Jurado played sheriff Slim Pickens' wife and partner in this melancholy look at the Old West. Determined and tough as nails, Jurado's character was clearly her screen husband's equal, and she had a very moving scene with Pickens as his character faced death. The film also featured Richard Jaekel, Chill Wills, Barry Sullivan, Jason Robards, and a horde of western character actors like R.G. Armstrong, L.Q. Jones, and Jack Elam.

> The film truly undermines the romantic gunplay of the classic western, emphasizing instead the basic amorality and essential illogic of human nature. And according to reports, Peckinpah was drunk and really moody through most of the making of the movie.

3. *The Badlanders* - 1958

Two men are released from the Arizona Territorial Prison at Yuma in

1898. One, the Dutchman (Alan Ladd), is out to get both gold and revenge from the people of a small mining town who had him imprisoned unjustly. The other, McBain (Ernest Borgnine), is just trying to go straight, but that is easier said than done once the Dutchman involves him in his gold theft scheme. McBain rescues a Mexican woman, Anita (Katy Jurado), when men accost her on the street. A grateful Anita invites McBain to stay in her place, and they become a couple.

The unique pairing of Alan Ladd and Ernest Borgnine actually works really well in this film, and the supporting cast includes Kent Smith, Nehemiah Persoff, and Anthony Caruso.

NOTE: Ernest Borgnine met his future wife Katy Jurado while working on this film. A reporter saw the two laughing over lunch one day and started a rumor that the two were involved romantically, which Borgnine insisted for the rest of his life was not true. The story persisted, though, and Borgnine's wife ended up divorcing him because of it. Ironically, he and Jurado grew closer and closer because of this trouble, and ended up marrying in 1959. But they only stayed married for about four years.

Ernest Borgnine and Katy Jurado in happier times

GOOD GUYS, BAD GUYS, AND SIDEKICKS IN WESTERN MOVIES

4. *Broken Lance* - 1954

Broken Lance has been covered in the section on Richard Widmark. Katy Jurado plays the wife of Spencer Tracy in this film. Robert Wagner plays Matt's son by the Native American princess, "Señora." (The townspeople call her Señora out of respect for Matt but not out of respect for her.) Ben (Richard Widmark), Mike (Hugh O'Brian), and Denny (Earl Holliman)—all Caucasian sons of Matt's first wife – have no respect or affection for either Senora Devereaux or son Joe. When Joe gets out of prison for taking the blame for a crime his father and brothers actually committed, he seeks revenge against the three brothers for essentially causing the death of their father. .

Somehow I find it hard to picture Robert Wagner being of mixed ethnicity, but Katy Jurado comes across pretty well in the part. In fact, she was good enough to be nominated for an Oscar for Best Supporting Actress, but lost out to Eva Marie Saint for *On the Waterfront*.

5. *One-Eyed Jacks* – 1961

One-Eyed Jacks has already been covered under the films of Slim Pickens. Suffice it to say that Katy Jurado does not shrink from her role as the wife of a very mean husband, played by Karl Malden. She confronts him effectively on several occasions during this film.

Summary

Katy Jurado was an actress who was much more than her image of a "Mexican spitfire." A really good actress, she was a leader in getting better parts for Hispanic actresses and paved the way for many of the Hispanic female starts of today. Most of her best roles, particularly at the beginning of her American career, were in western films.

6. Harry Carey (1878-1947)

Harry Carey – the western film star, not the baseball announcer who broadcast for the St. Louis Cardinals for most of his career and for the Chicago Cubs for the latter part of his career – was a famous leading man of early western films, and became a western character actor/supporting player in the 1930s and 40s when he was in his 50s and 60s. He was perhaps John Ford's favorite star, which was no easy matter giving Ford's general dislike of actors. Carey had an almost 40 year career in movies, and his son, Harry Carey, Jr. also became a leading supporting actor in western films.

My favorite Harry Carey talkie westerns were the following:
1. Red River
2. Angel and the Badman
3. The Shepherd of the Hills
4. Duel in the Sun
5. The Spoilers

Biography

Harry Carey, the silent film star and later B-movie cowboy and A-list character actor, was born about as far away from a western ranch as you can imagine. Born on January 16, 1878, in Bronx, NY, Henry DeWitt Carey II was the son of a prominent lawyer who was the president of a sewing machine company. Harry was educated at Hamilton Military Academy but turned down an appointment to West Point and instead appeared briefly as an actor in a stock company. He then returned to a more normal life and enrolled in New York University to learn the law in the hopes of following his father's career choice; however, his studies were interrupted by a severe case of pneumonia that resulted from a boating accident in Long Island Sound when he was 21 years old.

Carey's love of horses was instilled in him at a young age as he watched New York City's mounted policemen go through their paces in the 1880s, and while recuperating from pneumonia, he wrote a play, "Montana," about the Western frontier. He decided to star in his own creation, and the play proved a big success. Audiences were thrilled when Carey brought his horse onto the stage.

For three years Carey made quite a bit of money touring with "Montana." After that production was played out, he wrote another play, a Klondike tale entitled "Heart of Alaska," which was presented as "Two Women and that Man" on Broadway.

Discarding thoughts of following his father's footsteps and becoming a lawyer, Harry continued his involvement with acting, now well past the flirtation stage. Having lost his money on the "Alaska" play, Harry turned to the movies, the production of which was centered in the New York City metropolitan area at that time – not Hollywood. His first credited picture of any importance was Bill Sharkey's *Last Game* (1910). In 1911, with the help of famous actor Henry B. Walthall, Carey became part of the Biograph stock company. He began appearing in films for director D.W. Griffith, most memorably in *The Musketeers of Pig Alley* (1912), in which he played a hood in the 'hoods of New York. Carey's movie acting career was launched at the

Biograph studios in the Bronx, and he would eventually appear in almost 250 films and become a big star in silent film Westerns. Carey followed Griffith to Hollywood and appeared in his *The Battle of Elderbush Gulch* (1913) with Lillian Gish, Lionel Barrymore and a young stud whom Griffith would rename Elmo Lincoln, who would later become the first of the cinema Tarzans.

It was at Universal that Harry Carey became a silent film cowboy star, playing "Cheyenne Harry" in a series of two-reel westerns. In most of the films, his co-stars included the teen-aged Olive Golden as the love interest and Hoot Gibson as his young sidekick. The movies were made under the auspices of producer-director Francis Ford's shorts and serials department, and when Carey created his own unit, he took along Olive as his co-star and Ford's younger brother, Jack, as his director. Jack--the former John Feeney, late of Portland, Maine, thereafter to become renowned under the name John Ford—began his craft by directing 26 two-reel Westerns and features with Carey as 'Cheyenne Harry.' Carey eventually married Olive in 1920, who became known professionally as Olive Carey. They settled on a ranch in California's Santa Clarita Valley, near Saugus, in the San Francisquito Canyon. It was there that their son Harry Carey Jr. was born in 1921.

Carey's cowboys emphasized realism and as such were different from those of Ken Maynard and Tom Mix. Good with physical action, particularly involving his hands, Carey developed signature gestures such as the way he sat on a horse, a semi-slouch with his elbows resting on the saddle horn. Another signature was his holding his left forearm with his right. (His good friend John Wayne, who said that Harry Carey "was the greatest Western actor of all time," paid a tribute to him by using this trait at the end of John Ford's classic *The Searchers* (1956), when he walks away from the character played by Carey's widow Olive, and is framed by the doorway in the final scene of the film). By the end of the decade Carey was one of the highest paid western stars, earning $1,250 a week (approximately $15,400 in 2005 dollars) in those pre-income tax days. In 1922, when Universal decided to make Carey's sidekick Hoot Gibson its top Western star, Carey left the studio, thus ending his collaboration with John Ford.

When the sound era dawned at the end of the decade, Carey was still a top western star and very highly paid, but he did not enjoy the superstar status of Mix, Hoot Gibson, Maynard and Buck Jones. He also was 50 years old with a career stretching back 20 years to the days of the nickelodeon. Considering him passé, his studio (Pathe) failed to renew his contract. After a stretch on the vaudeville circuit, Carey returned to the movies and was demoted to supporting roles in the early talkies. Universal Studios head Irving Thalberg decided to give Carey a shot at sound cinema stardom in the new extravaganza he had planned and would personally produce (uncredited, as always, during his lifetime).

Carey's star assumed a new luster playing the lead role in MGM's "Great White Hunter" African epic *Trader Horn* (1931), in which he overpowered his second lead, Duncan Renaldo (who would later mature and ensure his cinematic and television immortality playing "The Cisco Kid"). His wife Olive also was in the picture. "Trader Horn" was a difficult shoot with scenes in Africa and Mexico, but it was a box-office hit, and Carey earned enough from the movie to rebuild and re-stock his ranch, which shortly thereafter was destroyed by fire and rebuilt.

Carey appeared in Motion Picture Herald's ranking of the top 10 of cowboy box office stars of 1937 and 1938, when he was past his prime as a cowboy star and began moving into other film genres. For example, Carey won an Academy Award nomination for his performance as the Vice President who was James Stewart's ally in the Frank Capra classic *Mr. Smith Goes to Washington* (1939). Though Carey lost the Oscar to Thomas Mitchell, who won playing the whiskey-besotted doctor in Ford's classic *Stagecoach* (1939), it was a nice gesture of respect from Hollywood to one of its own.

Carey appeared with John Wayne in the Technicolor picture *The Shepherd of the Hills* (1941) for Paramount and the two bonded, with Wayne becoming a sort of surrogate son with his own son away at war. Wayne, as a young Marion Morrison, had grown up watching the Carey "Cheyenne Harry" westerns, and he claimed that Carey and

Yakima Canutt were the only two cowboy actors he ever learned from. Carey and his wife invited Wayne into their extended family (Olive gave the Duke Carey's western memorabilia after his death). It was an association that continued onscreen, when Carey appeared memorably as Wayne's partner in *The Spoilers* (1942) and as a sympathetic marshal trailing Wayne in *Angel and the Badman* (1947) for Republic Pictures.

> Speaking of Yakima Canutt, starting out as a rodeo cowboy and then becoming a stuntman in silent westerns, Yakima Canutt later became famous as John Wayne's double, performing such dangerous stunts as jumping off the top of a cliff on horseback, leaping from a stagecoach onto its runaway team, being "shot" off a horse at full gallop and other such potentially life-threatening activities.

Yakima Canutt, John Wayne's double for most of his difficult stunts.

After World War II ended, Harry Carey Senior and Junior and The Duke finally appeared together in Howard Hawks' classic western *Red River* (1948) Sadly, it was the only film father and son were to make together, and they did not share any scenes. A smoker, Harry Carey developed emphysema and suffered from lung cancer. The ailing Carey, who had sold his ranch in 1944, continued to act, appearing in the Technicolor drama *Duel in the Sun* (1946) He also had an uncredited bit part in *The Babe Ruth Story* (1948), playing the manager of the St. Louis Cardinals, a stretch for a native New Yorker born in the borough the Yankees call home.

Harry Carey died on September 21, 1947, the causes of his death given as emphysema, lung cancer and coronary thrombosis. When he was interred in the Carey family mausoleum at Woodlawn Cemetery in The Bronx, New York, clad in a cowboy outfit, over 1,000 admirers turned out for the funeral.

John Ford dedicated his film *3 Godfathers* (1948), a remake of his 1916 film (*The Three Godfathers*) starring Carey--to Harry's memory. The dedication recognized a great Western star, one whom arguably represented the true 'Westerner' better than any other movie actor.

Awards and Recognition

Harry Carey was nominated for an Oscar for Best Supporting Actor for *Mr. Smith Goes to Washington*, a non-western film.

In 1976 he was inducted into the Western Performers Hall of Fame at the National Cowboy and Western Heritage Museum in Oklahoma City, OK. He was posthumously awarded a Golden Boot by the Motion Picture & Television Fund Foundation in 1991.

My Favorite Harry Carey Westerns

1. *Red River* – 1948

This film has already been discussed in the section on John Wayne and will be discussed again in the category of favorite westerns. In this film, Harry Carey played the part of Mr. Melville, the president of the Green River Trading Company, who buys all of John Wayne/Montgomery Clift's cattle after the long cattle ride from the Red River in Texas to Abilene, Kansas. Melville senses that there is going to be trouble between the Dunston (Wayne) and Garth (Clift) characters once Dunston gets into Abilene.

This was the next-to-last film made by Carey and an outstanding one. Carey does not come into the film until the last 30 minutes but has a significant role.

2. *Angel and the Badman* – 1947

In my opinion, a very nice and under-rated western starring John Wayne and Gail Russell and already discussed in the section on Wayne. Carey plays Marshal Wistful McClintock, who realizes that the Wayne character (Quirt Evans) has gone from a former deputy sheriff to the wrong side of the law and wonders why. He is continually watching (and predicting) for Quirt to make a mistake that will force McClintock to arrest him or even shoot him, but nonetheless hopes for the best for the likeable Quirt.

> Gail Russell represents one of the most tragic of all Hollywood stories. A local girl of stunning beauty, she was so nervous on screen that studio executives gave her alcohol to "settle her nerves." In her case, a terrible idea, since she became an alcoholic and died at the age of 36 of alcoholism. Two of her very best films were with John Wayne – this one and *Wake of the Red Witch* in 1948.

John Wayne and Gail Russell in *Angel and the Badman*

3. *The Shepherd of the Hills* – 1941

Harold Bell Wright's bestselling 1907 novel The Shepherd of the Hills had been previously filmed in 1919 and 1928 before Paramount offered the first talkie version in 1941. In one of his least typical roles, John Wayne plays a young Ozark backwoodsman forsworn to kill his father, who years earlier abandoned his mother. Against this personal crisis is played the larger drama of outsiders who threaten to push Wayne's friends and family off their land. Fate plays a hand when a mysterious stranger (Harry Carey) wanders into the community and becomes pretty much a mediator of disputes – he is the Shepherd of the Hills. Not at all the action picture one would expect from star John Wayne and director Henry Hathaway, *Shepherd of the Hills* moves at a leisurely pace, instead unfolding its story at a pace consistent with its slow-moving characters. The film's rich Technicolor photography adds to the restfully rustic ambience of this unusual entertainment.

This is one of Carey's best sound pictures as the title character, the *Shepherd of the Hills*.

4. *Duel in the Sun* – 1946

This film was already reviewed in the section on Gregory Peck. Carey has a small part as the friend of Lionel Barrymore, one of the central characters in the movie and the father of Gregory Peck and Lionel Barrymore. At this point in his career, Carey was settling for smaller character parts like this one.

5. *The Spoilers* – 1942

In Nome, Alaska, miner Roy Glennister (John Wayne) and his partner Dextry (Harry Carey), financed by saloon entertainer Cherry Malotte (Marlene Dietrich), fight to save their gold claim from crooked commissioner Alexander McNamara (Randolph Scott). Carey's character is Dextry, not Destry, and can Randolph Scott possibly be the villain? He was in this film.

In 1942, Wayne was still not yet the star that he would eventually become, so he received third billing behind Dietrich and Scott.

Summary

While the vast majority of Harry Carey's leading man roles were in silent films in the 1910's and 1920's, where he was a huge star, he played a number of mostly supporting roles in the next two decades. A truly revered actor by fellow actors and directors alike – including the cantankerous John Ford, who generally belittled actors – Carey was perhaps Ford's favorite. John Wayne was so devoted to Carey that in the closing scene of *The Searchers* with John Wayne framed in the doorway, Wayne holds his right elbow with his left hand in a pose that Carey fans would recognize as one that he often used. Wayne later stated he did it as a tribute to Carey.

Just remember that it's Harry Carey the western star, NOT Harry Caray, the baseball announcer.

Harry Caray leading the Wrigley Field faithful in yet another singing of Take Me Out to the Ballgame during the seventh inning.

7. Arthur Hunnicutt – 1910-1979

Now here's a guy who looks like someone you might actually find in the Old West – grizzled, plain-spoken, scruffy-looking Arthur Hunnicutt. But in real life, Arthur Hunnicutt was anything but the scraggly, unkempt hobo that he often appeared to be on the silver screen.

A veteran of 91 movies and television roles, including guest shots on shows like Bonanza, Laramie, Walt Disney's Wonderful World of Color, and even Perry Mason[33] – Hunnicutt looked so rural and

---

[33] "The Case of the Golden Oranges". For Amos Kenesaw Mountain Keller (Hunnicutt) to have been a veteran of the Spanish-American War (a.k.a. the War of 1898), as was claimed in the episode. he would have had to have been 80 or 90 years old. Arthur Hunnicutt was only in his fifties at the time

spoke with such a twangy voice that he was a natural for westerns. No clean-cut look for Mr. Hunnicutt, he looked, spoke, and acted more like post-Civil War western folks than probably any other American actor this side of Gabby Hayes.

My favorite Arthur Hunnicutt westerns, and he made a lot!
1. El Dorado
2. The Big Sky
3. The Last Command
4. The Tall T
5. The Lusty Men
6. Broken Arrow

Biography

A native of Gravelly, Arkansas, Arthur Lee Hunnicutt attended Arkansas State Teachers College but dropped out during his junior year when he ran out of money. He moved to Martha's Vineyard, Massachusetts, where he joined up with a theatre company. Moving to New York, he quickly found himself landing roles in Broadway productions. While touring as the lead actor in "Tobacco Road", he developed the country character he would later be typecast as throughout his career. Perhaps because of that, Hunnicutt often found himself cast as a character much older than himself.

Hunnicutt appeared in a number of films in the early 1940s before returning to the stage. Then in 1949 he moved back to Hollywood and resumed his film career. He played a long string of supporting role characters—sympathetic, wise rural types, as in *The Red Badge of Courage* (1951), *The Lusty Men* (1952), *The Kettles in the Ozarks* (1955), *The Last Command* (1955, as Davy Crockett), *The Tall T* (1957), *Cat Ballou* (1965, as Butch Cassidy), *El Dorado* (1966) and *The Adventures of Bullwhip Griffin*.

In 1952, he was nominated for an Academy Award for Best Supporting Actor in the Howard Hawks Western, *The Big Sky*.

Throughout the '50s, '60s and '70s, Hunnicutt made nearly 40 guest appearances in television programs. He made two memorable appearances on *Perry Mason* in 1963: playing orange grower Amos Kennesaw Mountain Keller in "The Case of the Golden Oranges," and prospector Sandy Bowen in "The Case of the Drowsy Mosquito." He also made guest appearances on *Bonanza*, *Gunsmoke*, *The Outer Limits*, *The Rifleman*, *Wanted: Dead or Alive* (TV series), *The Andy Griffith Show*, and *The Twilight Zone*. In one of his last movies, *Moonrunners* (1975)—the precursor to *The Dukes of Hazzard*—he played the original Uncle Jesse.

He was married once to Pauline Lile. In his later years, Hunnicutt served as Honorary Mayor of Northridge, California. In his later years, he developed tongue cancer. He died in 1979 and is buried in the Coop Prairie Cemetery in Mansfield, Arkansas.

Will Hutchins – TV's "Sugarfoot" – had this to say about Hunnicutt:" I hugely enjoyed working with Arthur Hunnicutt on the pilot show of "Sugarfoot." He was a lanky, shaggy, bearded philosopher with a long, mournful twang. Told me he missed winning an Oscar for his work in "The Big Sky" by one vote to "Viva Zapata's" Anthony Quinn. If I'd been an Academy member in 1952 Arthur and Anthony would have tied. Arthur was a mellow fellow and he got mellower as the hours passed. I figured he was on a health kick. He ate oranges all day. Turned out he laced 'em with vodka via a hypodermic needle—Ol' Hunnicutt was a walking screwdriver."

Awards and Recognition

Arthur Hunnicutt was an Oscar nominee for Best Supporting Actor for *The Big Sky* in 1952. He lost out to Anthony Quinn in *Viva Zapata*!

My Favorite Arthur Hunnicutt Westerns

1. *El Dorado* – **1967**

This western is essentially a remake of *Rio Bravo*, with Robert Mitchum playing the Dean Martin part, James Caan taking the place of Ricky Nelson, Arthur Hunnicutt replacing Walter Brennan, and John Wayne replacing – well, John Wayne.

Hired gunman Cole Thornton (John Wayne) turns down a job with Bart Jason (Ed Asner before the Mary Tyler Moore show) - as it would mean having to go up against an old sheriff friend (Robert Mitchum). Some months later he finds out the lawman is on the bottle and a top gunfighter is heading his way to help Jason. Along with young Mississippi (James Caan), handy with a knife and now armed with a weird shotgun, Cole returns to help his old friend. Hunnicutt is Bull, a deputy sheriff. A strong supporting cast includes Paul Fix, Charlene Holt, Christopher George, and R.G. Armstrong.

2. *The Big Sky* – 1952

Arthur Hunnicutt's Oscar nominated performance is a good one. *The Big Sky* is a 1952 American Western film directed by Howard Hawks, based on the novel of the same name. The cast includes Kirk Douglas, Dewey Martin, Elizabeth Threatt and Hunnicutt.

In 1832, Jim Deakins (Kirk Douglas) is traveling in the wilderness when he encounters an initially hostile Boone Caudill (Dewey Martin). However, they soon become good friends. They head to the Missouri River in search of Boone's uncle, Zeb Calloway (Arthur Hunnicutt). They find him when they are tossed in jail for brawling with fur traders of the Missouri River Company. When 'Frenchy' Jourdonnais (Steven Geray) comes to bail Zeb out, Zeb talks him into paying for Jim and Boone too.

The two men join an expedition organized by Zeb and Frenchy to travel 2,000 miles up the river to trade with the Blackfoot Indians, in competition with the Missouri Company. Zeb has brought along Teal Eye (Elizabeth Threatt), a pretty Blackfoot woman Zeb found several years before after she had escaped from an enemy tribe. Zeb intends to use her as a hostage, as she is the daughter of a chief. On the journey, they encounter another Blackfoot Zeb knows, Poordevil

(Hank Worden); they take him along. And that is just the beginning of the fun.

Though not considered among Hawks' major achievements by most critics, the film was chosen by film historian/critic for the *Chicago Reader* Jonathan Rosenbaum for his alternative list of the Top 100 American Films.

> Hank Worden is a very interesting actor and could have easily been in my book. He generally played western characters who were of less than average intelligence, yet in real life Hank was trained as an engineer and attended Stanford and the University of Nevada. He made 17 westerns with John Wayne, including *The Searchers* and *Red River*. Worden lived to the ripe old age of 91.

Hank Worden from *The Searchers*. "Ol' Mose knows," as they said in the film.

3. *The Last Command* – 1955

In this interesting retelling of the fall of the Alamo, Arthur Hunnicutt plays a very different looking Davy Crockett from what we were used to seeing when we were growing up– Fess Parker, and John Wayne. Crockett was 50 years old during the battle and probably looked a lot more like Hunnicutt than like Parker or even Wayne.

During the Texas War of Independence of 1836 American frontiersman and pioneer Jim Bowie (Sterling Hayden) pleads for caution with the Texicans in dealing with nearby Mexico. But they don't heed his advice since he's a Mexican citizen, married to the daughter of the Mexican vice-governor of the province and a friend to General Santa Anna since the days they had fought together for Mexico's independence. However, after serving as president for 22 years, Santa Anna has become powerful and arrogant. He rules Mexico with an iron fist and will not allow Texas to self-govern. Bowie sides with the Texans in their bid for independence and urges a cautious strategy, given Santa Anna's power and cunning.

Despite the disagreement between the Texicans and Bowie regarding the right strategy, they ask Bowie to lead them in a last ditch stand, at the Alamo, against General Santa Anna's numerically superior forces – something in the neighborhood of 5,000 against 180. Richard Carlson plays Colonel Travis with J. Carrol Naish – of Irish decent, but who played a lot of Latin parts because of his looks – as General Santa Ana. Overall, a pretty good retelling of the story of the Alamo with a more realistic-looking Davy Crockett than we usually see in films. .

Arthur Hunnicutt as Davy Crockett in *The Last Command*,

with Richard Carlson as Colonel Travis second from left. That's what Davy Crockett probably looked like by the time he got to Texas.

4. *The Tall T* – 1957

Based on a story by Elmore Smith, and directed by Budd Boetticher, *The Tall T* is a very good Randolph Scott western – already covered under Scott.

Having lost his horse in a bet, Pat Brennan (Randolph Scott) hitches a ride with a stagecoach carrying two older newlyweds, Willard and Doretta Mims (John Hubbard and Maureen O'Sullivan). At the next station the coach and its passengers fall into the hands of a trio of outlaws headed by a man named Usher – Richard Boone, with Henry Silva and Skip Homeier as his younger sidekicks. When Usher learns that Doretta is the daughter of a rich copper-mine owner, he decides to hold her for ransom. Tension builds over the next 24 hours as Usher awaits a response to his demands and as a romantic attachment grows between Brennan and Doretta.

Arthur Hunnicutt plays the station master who has a rather untimely exit fairly early in the movie. Richard Boone, in particular, is good in his role. While he is clearly the villain and a murderer, the audience has the impression that, had he gotten a break or two earlier in life, things may have turned out differently for him.

5. *The Lusty Men* – 1952

This film is covered under the films of Arthur Kennedy in the Bad Guys section. Kennedy (Wes Merritt) has a much bigger role than Arthur Hunnicutt's character in this film.

Jeff's friend Booker Davis (Arthur Hunnicutt), once a champion competitor himself, is now a crippled old man with little to show for his efforts. And Wes' wife, played by Susan Hayward, does not want her husband ending up in the same situation as Davis.

GOOD GUYS, BAD GUYS, AND SIDEKICKS IN WESTERN MOVIES

> Two Arthurs in the same movie, Wow! That is a rarity. Too bad they could not add Arthur Hill to the cast. Or made it a musical and added dance instructor Arthur Murray.

6. *Broken Arrow* - 1950

Broken Arrow is an excellent western, one of the few made in that era that is sympathetic to the plight of Native Americans. The film stars James Stewart as peacemaker Tom Jeffords, with Jeff Chandler as Cochise and Debra Paget as an Indian princess.

By 1870, there has been 10 years of war between settlers and Cochise's Apaches. Ex-soldier Tom Jeffords saves the life of an Apache boy and starts to wonder if Indians have a legitimate gripe against the government, after all; soon, he determines to use this chance to make himself an ambassador. Against all odds, his solitary mission into Cochise's stronghold opens a dialogue. Opportunity knocks when the President sends General Howard with orders to conclude peace. But even with Jeffords's luck, the deep grievance and hatred on both sides makes tragic failure all too likely. Hunnicutt plays mail superintendent Milt Duffield.

It seemed to me that Debra Paget – real name Debralee Griffin – played a lot of Native American princesses/women. Must be the high cheekbones, I guess. As of the writing of this book, she is 83. She was the romantic interest of James Stewart in this film, even though at the time, he was 42 and she was 17.

Summary

Again, I always liked Arthur Hunnicutt, from the first time I saw him on film – probably in *The Last Command* – and said "Who is this guy?" He was a good actor, a good person, and really looked the part of someone who had actually lived in the post-Civil War West.

Bad Guys

1. Dan Duryea – 1907-1968

Whether he was in westerns or gangster/film noir films (his two specialties), Dan Duryea was one of the meanest, nastiest, rottenest, despicable characters you would ever want to meet onscreen, and one of the nicest, most genuine guys you would ever meet offscreen.

As the International Movie Data Base (IMDB) put it so perfectly, "Dan Duryea was definitely the man you went to the movies for and loved to hate. His sniveling, deliberately taunting demeanor and snarling flat, nasal tones set the actor apart from other similar slimeballs of the 1940s and 1950s." [34] And I could not think of a better one-word description of his character than "slimeball."

---

[34] IMDB page on Dan Duryea

While Dan Duryea made a lot of gangster/film noir pictures, my favorite Duryea westerns are the following:

1. Winchester '73
2. Al Jennings of Oklahoma
3. Along Came Jones
4. Night Passage
5. Black Bart
6. Ride Clear of Diablo

Biography

Dan Duryea actually got his start, along with so many other actors of that era, as a stage actor who moved to films fairly early on in his career with no particular difficulties at all.

Born in White Plains, New York, on January 23, 1907, the son of a textile salesman, Dan showed an early interest in acting and was a member of his hometown high school's drama club. Majoring in English at Cornell University and president of his university's drama club, he had a career shift after deciding that the advertising business was perhaps a more level-headed pursuit than acting. However, after suffering a mild heart attack in his late 20s, he gave up his idea of a business career to return to his first love. In the long run, it seemed to work out for Dan and for moviegoers in general.

Following some summer stock experience, Duryea made his Broadway debut in a bit part in the Depression-era play "Dead End" in 1935. He moved to the leading role of Gimpy later in the show's year-long run. But his best role on stage was being cast as nephew Leo in "The Little Foxes" starring Tallulah Bankhead in 1939. After playing the part for the entire Broadway run, he then joined the national tour of the play. Fortunately, when Samuel Goldwyn bought the film rights, Duryea was included in the cast and made his screen debut in *The Little Foxes* (1941) with Bette Davis replacing Bankhead as the lead character, Regina.

As a result, Duryea continued in films and never returned to the Broadway stage. Seldom venturing into the "nice guy" arena, audiences continued to enjoy his perpetual mean streak and waited anxiously for his character to get what he deserved by the end of the movie, whether in westerns or crime dramas and whether by gunshot, poison or even the electric chair. Co-starring in "A"-quality films at the onset, he played a henchman of Dana Andrews in Billy Wilder's *Ball of Fire* (1941) opposite Gary Cooper and Barbara Stanwyck, then played Cooper's nemesis again as both a smart aleck reporter in *The Pride of the Yankees* (1942) and as a gunslinger who takes pot shots at him in *Along Came Jones* (1945).

He continued to harass other stars too, including Edward G. Robinson in the dark and superb Fritz Lang films *The Woman in the Window* (1944) (a blackmailer) and *Scarlet Street* (1945) (an art forger). A really good Dan Duryea non-western of the period is *Lady on a Train*, a murder mystery starring Deanna Durbin. Everyone, including Durbin, assumes that the one brother – Duryea – is the murderer, when it is seemingly nice guy brother Ralph Bellamy who is the real murderer. Nice job of casting by the director!

Duryea signed with Universal at the peak of his career, but this post-WWII move resulted in a lack of quality films. More often than not he found himself mired in such "B" grade outings as *Black Bart* (1948) and *River Lady* (1948). He also appeared in light comedy as well, as in the case of his starring butler role in *White Tie and Tails* (1946), where he is somewhat overshadowed by Ella Raines and William Bendix.

"Once a scoundrel, always a scoundrel" was his onscreen motto. He performed fine work in *Another Part of the Forest* (1948), this time playing Oscar Hubbard in a prequel to "The Little Foxes", and in *Criss Cross* (1949), where he gets to kill both Burt Lancaster and Yvonne De Carlo. Very few people ever got the best of Lancaster in his films.

While most of Duryea's 1950s films were considered average, more sympathetic roles also surfaced for him in the form of *Chicago Calling* (1951), *Thunder Bay* (1953), *Battle Hymn* (1957) and *Kathy O'* (1958).

Like many actors of his generation the 1950s also saw him move to a large extent towards roles on TV. This included his own brief series "China Smith" (1952)/"The New Adventures of China Smith" (1954), along with guest appearances on such popular series as "Wagon Train" (1957).

Duryea's movie reputation as a villain did not extend into his personal life. Long married (from 1932) to Helen Bryan and a family man at heart (he was once a scoutmaster and PTA parent!), he had two children. One of them, Peter Duryea became an actor for about a decade in the mid-'60s; father and son, in fact, appeared together in the western films *Taggart* (1964) and *The Bounty Killer* (1965). A second son, Richard, became a talent agent.

Duryea found good parts hard to find in his final years and even went overseas to drum up some work in European low-budgeters, including "spaghetti westerns." In 1967 he appeared in *Winchester 73* (1967), a made-for-TV remake of one of his more popular 1950s western films of the same name (1950). Another television acting job late in his career came in the recurring form of shady conman Eddie Jacks on the popular night-time soap serial *Peyton Place* (1964).

Duryea's wife Helen died in January of 1967 of heart problems and Dan passed away a year later at age 61 after being diagnosed with cancer. *The New York Times* tellingly noted the passing of a "heel with sex appeal." They are buried together in Forest Lawn Cemetery in Los Angeles.

Awards and Recognition

Surprisingly, Dan Duryea was never nominated for an Oscar. He does, however, have a star on the Hollywood Walk of Fame as of 1960.

My Favorite Dan Duryea Westerns

1. *Winchester '73* – 1950

See the write-up under James Stewart for a general review of the film. Dan Duryea plays a baddy named Waco Johnnie Dean (as I said earlier, it should have been Wacko Johnnie Dean). Dean is one of the many characters that Lin (Stewart) comes across as he pursues the Winchester rifle that was stolen by his brother, played by Stephen McNally. Waco is certainly the nastiest of the characters that Stewart comes across in his pursuit of the rifle, and of course, these two do not exactly see eye to eye on anything, including Shelley Winters as the misguided wife of Steve (Charles Drake), who also has an unfortunate run-in with Waco Johnnie.

Duryea is simply beyond nasty in this great western film, and he really hates and/or mistrusts everyone, including the members of his own gang of thieves and murderers.

Dan Duryea attempting to charm Shelley Winters is his usual less than sophisticated manner. (Scaring the daylights out of her.)

2. *Al Jennings of Oklahoma* – 1951

This film is a big unusual as Duryea plays real life outlaw Al Jennings in a rather sympathetic role. In this film, the four Jennings brothers are actually lawyers. When Al's brother is murdered, Al goes after the murderer. He outdraws him but a witness says it was murder. In the process of escaping the sheriff, Jennings takes refuge on a cattle ranch only to learn all the ranch hands are actually cattle rustlers. With a price on his head, Al joins them and becomes an outlaw. His fame grows as does the reward for his capture. Jennings is treated as a rather sympathetic character in this film. [35] Gale Storm (television's "My Little Margie"), Dick Foran, and Guinn "Big Boy" Williams co-star.

The real Al Jennings. I have seen meaner looking western outlaws, I will admit.

---

[35] The subject of a story by the writer O. Henry, the real Al Jennings wrote his autobiography on which this film was made. He actually ran for governor of Oklahoma as a democrat, which of course means he lost. Then he went out to Hollywood and made western films, of course. He was advisor on this film, in fact. He apparently was much better at embellishing his exploits as an outlaw than he was an outlaw, where he was not very successful at all. Al Jennngs died in 1961 at the age of 98 – not bad for a western bank robber.

3. *Along Came Jones* – 1945

See the write-up of this film under the section on Gary Cooper. Duryea plays notorious gunman Monte Jarrad, whom Cooper is mistaken for. When Cherry, Jarrad's girlfriend, meets Cooper (Jones), she starts to realize that maybe Duryea's character is not such an ideal suitor, after all.

> "Along Came Jones" is also the name of a 1959 song by The Coasters, which has absolutely nothing whatsoever to do with the plot of this western.

4. *Night Passage* – 1957

A very under-appreciated western, in my opinion. The workers on the railroad haven't been paid in months --- that's because Whitey Harbin (Duryea, of course) and his gang, including fast-shooting, dangerous, but likeable Utica Kid (Audie Murphy), keep holding up the train for its payroll. Grant McLaine (James Stewart), a former railroad employee who was fired in disgrace, is recruited to take the payroll through under cover. A young boy (Brandon De Wilde) and a shoebox figure into the plot when Whitey's gang tries to hold up the train and Grant and the Utica Kid (who are actually brothers who followed separate paths) meet again to settle an old score. James Stewart even plays the accordion and sings "You can't get far without a railroad" and "Follow the River." What more could you want?

Audie Murphy certainly could have been in the book – he made enough western films – but I just never liked him all that much. He was, however, the most decorated soldier in World War II, being awarded the Medal of Honor and 32 other awards for bravery.

Audie Murphy died in a private plane crash in 1971 at 47.

5. *Black Bart* - **1948**

Black Bart is another film with Dan Duryea in a starring rather than supporting role as the title character, Black Bart. And another true-life story, or at least a reasonably true story.

Outlaw Charlie Boles (Dan Duryea) leaves former partners Lance (Jeffrey Lynn) and Jersey (Percy Kilbride) and heads for California, where the Gold Rush is beginning. Soon, a lone gunman in black is robbing Wells Fargo gold shipments. One fateful day, the stage he robs carries old friends Lance and Jersey..and notorious dancer Lola Montez (Yvonne De Carlo), coming to perform in Sacramento. Black Bart and Lance become rivals for both Lola's favors and Wells Fargo's gold. The supporting cast is a good one – including Frank Lovejoy and John McIntire.

In case the name of Percy Kilbride sounds familiar, he played Pa Kettle in the Ma and Pa Kettle film series.

Previous Page. Marjorie Main and Percy Kilbride as Ma and Pa Kettle.

6. *Ride Clear of Diablo* - 1954

Railroad surveyor Clay O'Mara (Audie Murphy) goes after the rustlers who murdered his father and brother. Along the way, he teams up with outlaw Whitey Kincade (Duryea) who helps Murphy only to see how long the tenderfoot lasts. Outwitting several attempts on his life engineered by the crooked lawyer who set up his family, Murphy and a wounded Kincade face the gang. Duryea, wanting to protect Murphy and redeem himself, goes down shooting. Duryea is the outlaw turned good guy in this Audie Murphy western.

Summary

Dan Duryea was a versatile supporting actor, playing villains and heels in a wide variety of westerns and crime dramas/film noir. In real life, on the other hand, he was about as nice a guy as you could find anywhere. For an example of Duryea as a heavy in film noir, I recommend *Too Late for Tears*, where he plays opposite femme fatale Lizabeth Scott.

A very solid western baddie, who definitely belongs in this book.

2. Neville Brand – 1920-1992

Neville Brand played in tons of movies and television series (138 roles, to be exact). While some actors alternated between playing the hero and the villain – think of Richard Widmark and Dan Duryea, for example – Neville Brand was almost always cast as the heel. While he was in many war movies and crime dramas, I remember him particularly for his contributions to western films. A good actor, he was a highly decorated war hero, serving in many battles in the European theater during World War II. Oh, and he also was the guy who killed Elvis Presley in The King's first movie, *Love Me Tender*.

He was often cast as the thug who did the dirty work for the brainer, white collared villain.

My favorite Neville Brand westerns are:

1. The Last Sunset

2. The Tin Star
3. Badman's Country
4. Gun Fury
5. The Man from the Alamo
6. The Charge at Feather River

Biography

One of seven children, Neville Brand was born to Leo and Helen Brand on August 13th, 1920, in Griswold, Iowa. At the age of seven, he and his family moved to Kewanee, Illinois, where he grew up, graduated from high school, and entered the Illinois National Guard on October 23rd, 1939, as a private with Company F, 129th Infantry. Eighteen months later, Corporal Brand was inducted into U.S. military service with the 129th.

Neville Brand eventually departed for the European Theater of Operations on December 9th, 1944, and arrived there on December 16th. Relatively little is known of his nine months and nineteen days overseas, but his official military records reflect that Neville Brand participated in the Ardennes, Rhineland, and Central European campaigns, and received the Silver star while convalescing at the 21st General Hospital for gallantry in combat. His other medals and decorations are the Purple Heart, the Good Conduct Medal, the American Defense Service Ribbon, the European/African/Middle Eastern Theater Ribbon with three Battle Stars, one Overseas Service Bar, one Service Stripe, and the Combat Infantryman's Badge – quite a record. In a rare 1966 interview in which he consented to speak of his wartime service, Brand recalled how he earned his Silver Star when his unit came under intense fire from German machine guns located within a hunting lodge. "I must have flipped my lid," he said, for "I decided to go into that lodge." Disregarding his own safety, he worked his way around to the rear of the lodge/command post, burst in through the back, and single-handedly dispatched the enemy inside the lodge.

Later, on April 7th, 1945, exactly one month and a day before the official German surrender, Sergeant Brand was wounded in action by the Weser River. Felled by a gunshot to his upper right arm, and pinned down by withering enemy ground fire, Brand lay there slowly bleeding to death. "I knew I was dying," he said, "It was a lovely feeling, like being half-loaded." Rescued and treated, Brand was evacuated to a military hospital and, on September 17th, 1945, he departed for the United States. Less than a month later, Staff Sergeant Neville Brand was honorably discharged from the U.S. Army at Fort Sheridan, Illinois.[36] After his discharge, Neville Brand studied acting under the G.I. Bill, played in many theatrical productions, and appeared in one of his first films as a sadistic hoodlum opposite Edmond O'Brien in the 1950 production of *D.O.A.* Also among his earliest films was the Oscar-winning *Stalag 17* (1953).

His heavy features and gravelly voice made Brand a natural tough guy. "With this kisser, I knew early in the game I wasn't going to make the world forget Clark Gable," he once told a reporter. He played Al Capone in *The George Raft Story* (1961), *The Scarface Mob* (1959), and TV's *The Untouchables* (1959). Among his other memorable roles are the sympathetic guard in *Birdman of Alcatraz* (1962) and the representative of rioting convicts in *Riot in Cell Block 11* (1954). Perhaps his best-known role was that of the soft-hearted, loud-mouthed, none-too-bright but very effective Texas Ranger Reese Bennett of *Backtrack!* (1969), *Three Guns for Texas* (1968), and TV's *Laredo* (1965).

Over a career of roughly thirty-five years, Neville Brand consistently delivered outstanding performances on the stage, television and film, winning the prestigious Sylvania Award in 1958 for his performance in "All the King's Men." But I remember him most for his great western roles. Despite his gruff exterior, he was described by most as an actor's actor, very cooperative and easy to get along with; and his peers respected his work a great deal.

---

[36] From Neville Brand: Setting the Record Straight, by Robert E. Witter

Outside of acting, he was married three times and had three children. He was also an avid reader, and owned at one time one of the largest collections of books in a private library in the country, with over 30,000 books at one time. Unfortunately, Brand's home was destroyed by fire, and most of his personal mementoes (and cherished books) were lost. Some years later, reclusive and enduring a protracted struggle with emphysema, alcohol, and post traumatic stress disorder, Neville Brand passed away on April 16th, 1992, at Sutter General Hospital in Sacramento, California. His ashes are interred at East Lawn Memorial Park, Sacramento, California, in a vessel shaped like a book, with his name engraved on the spine.

Awards and Recognition

In addition to his military honors, Neville Brand was nominated for a BAFTA award[37] as Best Foreign Actor for his performance in *Riot in Cell Block 11* in 1954.

My Favorite Neville Brand Westerns

1. *The Last Sunset* – 1953

A good western of the early 1960's with two big stars in lead roles – Rock Hudson and Kirk Douglas. Brendan O'Malley (Kirk Douglas) arrives at the Mexican home of old flame Belle Breckenridge (an always gorgeous Dorothy Malone) to find her married to a drunkard (Joseph Cotten) getting ready for a cattle drive to Texas. Hot on O'Malley's heels is lawman Dana Stribling (Rock Hudson) who has a personal reason for getting him back into his jurisdiction. Both men join Breckenridge and his wife on the cattle drive. As they near Texas, tensions mount, not the least of which is because Stribling is starting to court Belle and O'Malley is increasingly drawn to her daughter Missy (Carol Lynley), and we learn what the reason for the attraction is as the film progresses. Neville Brand plays one of three

---

[37] BAFTA is the British Academy of Film and Television Arts, the equivalent of the Oscars and Emmys in this country.

GOOD GUYS, BAD GUYS, AND SIDEKICKS IN WESTERN MOVIES

hired hands – Jack Elam is another – who try unsuccessfully to abduct Belle and her daughter.

A good western with a twist at the end. The screenplay was written by Dalton Trumbo after his return off the Hollywood blacklist for having communist sympathies, and produced by Kirk Douglas' production company.

> Dalton Trumbo was a famed Hollywood screenwriter who was blacklisted in the late 1940's for being a member of the communist party. He worked under assumed names for several years before a very courageous Kirk Douglas gave him full screenwriting credit for a film you may have heard of, *Spartacus*, in 1960. Bryan Cranston portrayed him in the 2015 film, *Trumbo*. Cranston received an Oscar nomination for his portrayel of Dalton Trumbo.

2. *The Tin Star* – 1957

Veteran bounty-hunter Morg Hickman (Henry Fonda) rides into a troubled town on the brink of disaster. The sheriff has been killed, and young inexperienced Ben Owens (Tony Perkins) is named a temporary replacement until a permanent sheriff can be found. Ben wants to be that permanent replacement, so he needs to impress the townspeople. When he finds that Morg was a sheriff for a long time before he became a bounty-hunter, he asks the older man to teach him the tricks of the trade. Morg thinks that being a sheriff is a foolish goal, but agrees to teach Ben to handle people, more important to a sheriff's success than handling a gun. The cast also includes Betsy Palmer, John McIntyre, and Neville Brand as Bart Bogardus, naturally the villain, a town bully and an Indian hater. This film is a gem that is built more on relationships than constant action.

GOOD GUYS, BAD GUYS, AND SIDEKICKS IN WESTERN MOVIES

In my mind, Betsy Palmer is known primarily for two roles: as a panelist on the television show "I've Got a Secret", and as Jason Vorhees' mother in the film *Friday the 13th*. She was a Chicagoan – like me - whose real name was Patricia Betsy Hrunek, a Czech, also like me. She died in 2015 at the age of 88.

3. *Badman's Country* – 1958

Not a great western by any means, but an interesting one involving real western heroes and villains. Pat Garrett (George Montgomery) arrives in Abilene where he catches five of Butch Cassidy's (Neville Brand as Butch) gang. He calls in Wyatt Earp (Buster Crabbe), Buffalo Bill (Malcolm Atterbury) and Bat Masterson (Gregory Walcott) and they learn there is a half million dollar shipment of money arriving by train and Cassidy is amassing enough men to take it. They also realize he has tapped the telegraph line and they send a false message saying the money is already in the Abilene bank. But the townspeople not only refuse to fight but they release the prisoners trying to avoid a gunfight in their town.

A decent enough western starring a couple of B-western movie stars in Montgomery and Crabbe. However, although the plot has well-known actual western figures Pat Garrett, Wyatt Earp, Bat Masterson and Buffalo Bill fighting Butch Cassidy's gang. In reality by the time Cassidy had gathered his now-famous Hole-in-the-Wall Gang, including the Sundance Kid – played by "Gilligan's Island's" Russell

Johnson in this film - Garrett was dead, Buffalo Bill was touring in his Wild West show, Earp was prospecting for gold in Alaska and Masterson was a sportswriter for a newspaper in New York City. Oh, well, anything with Buster Crabbe and Neville Brand in it is OK by me.

You have probably seen this fellow in dozens of westerns, plus *North By Northwest*, *The Birds*, and *Perry Mason*, and wondered who he was. It's Malcolm Atterbury, born in that old western town of Philadelphia, Pennsylvania. He played in five episodes of *Perry Mason* alone, plus many other television roles.

4. *Gun Fury* – 1953

A western made in 3-D. After a stagecoach holdup, Frank Slayton (Philip Carey)'s notorious gang leave Ben Warren (Rock Hudson) for dead and head off with his fiancée (Donna Reed). Warren follows, and although none of the townspeople he comes across are prepared to help, he recruits two others who have sworn revenge on the ruthless Slayton. Supporting cast members include Brand, Lee Marvin, and Leo Gordon.

5. *The Man from the Alamo* – 1953

Already covered in the section on Glenn Ford, who plays the lone survivor of the Alamo. Neville Brand plays Dawes, a member of Victor Jory's gang of vigilantes who is in prison with Ford and recruits him – so he thinks – to the gang after they break out of prison. As always, Brand is the slimy villain who meets his end.

6. *The Charge at Feather River* - 1953

The plot of this 3-D film involves an overland journey through hostile Cheyenne territory to rescue two white women captured by the Cheyenne. One has turned renegade and is not anxious to be rescued as she is about to be married to Chief Thunder Hawk. Vera Miles dies and the cavalry comes to the rescue in the nick of time by a stream called Feather River. And since it is a 3-D film, knives, arrows, spears and tomahawks all come flying at the audience. And Frank Lovejoy discourages a rattlesnake with tobacco juice and even gets off a shot into the audience.

Guy Madison plays the hero along with a cast that includes the aforementioned Vera Miles and Frank Lovejoy, plus Dick Wesson, Steve Brodie, Lane Chandler, James Brown, and Neville Brand as members of the cavalry defending the river.

Madison took time off from his role as TV's Wild Bill Hickok (1951-1958) to play the hero in this and other films during that period of time.

> Guy Madison's real name was Robert Moseley, and the story goes that he changed his name to Guy Madison after seeing a Dolly Madison cake wagon pass by. What would have happened if he had seen an Oscar Meyer truck go by? Or a FED EX truck, by today's standards?

Guy Madison, handsome star of many westerns and also television's Wild Bill Hickok.

Summary

Neville Brand was a major villain in westerns, war movies, and crime dramas – he played Al Capone on three different occasions. I am still overwhelmed by the fact that he was such an avid reader and owned one of the largest private libraries of any private U.S. citizen at one time. I would have expected that of someone like Claude Rains, but not Neville Brand.

3. John Ireland - 1914-1992

Handsome John Ireland alternated between being the good guy and the bad guy in a wide variety of films – westerns, war movies, and crime dramas immediately come to mind. For example, he was Spartacus' best friend Crixus in the 1960 version of *Spartacus*, and was the good-guy reporter in *All the King's Men*, with Broderick Crawford as Willie Stark, based on the life of Huey Long. But he could also be a meanie, and played part of Ike Clanton's gang in two movies about the OK Corral gunfight, *My Darling Clementine* and *Gunfight at the OK Corral*. He was a sympathetic character in some westerns, including *Red River*, and a baddie in others. In a career of just over 200 film and television roles, I guess that is bound to happen.

My favorite John Ireland westerns were:
1. My Darling Clementine
2. Gunfight at the O.K. Corral
3. Red River
4. I Shot Jesse James
5. Vengeance Valley
6. Bushwackers
7. Gunslinger

Biography

Born in Vancouver, British Columbia, Canada on January 30, 1914, John Ireland was raised in New York. When Ireland was still a child, his parents – a horse breeder and a school teacher – moved the family first to San Francisco, and later to Harlem in New York City. While attending summer camps during his teen years, Ireland became a promising swimmer, and after leaving high school, he used his aquatic prowess to perform underwater stunts at a local carnival, where he also worked as a barker – think Billy Bigelow from *Carousel*. With this background he was able to move into the New York theater scene, often appearing in minor roles in Broadway plays. His first big break in motion pictures came in 1945 when he appeared as Windy the introspective letter-writing G.I. in the classic war epic *A Walk in the Sun*.

> I have seen *A Walk in the Sun* several times, and it is a really good, underappreciated WWII film. In the 1943 invasion of Italy, one American platoon lands, digs in, then makes its way inland to blow up a bridge next to a fortified farmhouse, as tension and casualties mount. Plus, they have lost all the officers, so Sergeant Bill Tyne – Dana Andrews in a terrific role – is forced to assume command. A great cast, in addition to Andrews and Ireland, includes Richard Conte, Lloyd Bridges, Sterling Holloway, Norman Lloyd, and even Huntz Hall of The Bowery Boys.

After that breakthrough role, Ireland was often featured (mostly as a villain) in several films. In 1949, he was nominated for best supporting actor for his role as the reporter in *All the King's Men*

(1949), based loosely on the life of Louisiana governor Huey Long. During the early 1950s, Ireland often starred as the emoting, brooding hero, although almost exclusively in "B" pictures. In 1953, with his son Peter Ireland and wife, Joanne Dru, Ireland co-produced and co-directed the western mini-classic *Hannah Lee: An American Primitive* (aka *Outlaw Territory*) – one of his two directorial efforts.

From the mid-'50s on, he appeared mainly in Italian "quickie" features and showed up occasionally in supporting roles in major films like *Spartacus* (1960)). Occasionally, his name was mentioned in tabloids of the times, in connection with young starlets, namely Natalie Wood, Barbara Payton, and Sue Lyon. He also attracted controversy by dating 16 year old actress Tuesday Weld when he was 45, then saying he would have married her except for her age and her mother.[38] But he reportedly also had an affair with seasoned actress Joan Crawford while on the set of *Queen Bee* in 1955. A decade later, Ireland and Crawford would co-star again in William Castle's horror flick *I Saw What You Did*. His "dallying" may actually have cost him larger roles in a few of his movies, as in *Red River*.

Ireland was set to play the role of the patriarch on the Ponderosa in "Bonanza: The Next Generation" (1988) but the series was not picked up. In addition to *Hannah Lee: An American Primitive*, his best work in the 50s was in *Little Big Horn* (1951) and *The Bushwhackers* (also 1951). In his later years, he owned and operated a tiny restaurant, Ireland's, in Santa Barbara, California.

The actor was married three times; first from 1940–1949, to Elaine Sheldon, by whom he had two sons named John and Peter. Then, from 1949-1957, to Joanne Dru. Finally, from 1962 until his death, to Daphne Myrick Cameron, with whom he had a daughter named Daphne and a son named Cameron.

John Ireland passed away from leukemia in March of 1992 at the age of 78.

---

[38] From John Ireland, *Outside of the Norm*

While he was a respected actor in American and Italian films, plus television, John Ireland's career was also unusual and often frustrating, consisting primarily of supporting roles in major productions and starring roles in minor films.

Awards and Recognition

John Ireland was nominated for an Oscar for Best Supporting Actor in the 1949 film *All the King's Men*. He also received a Golden Boot award in 1980 for his overall contribution to western films.

John Ireland and second wife, actress Joanne Dru, in happier times.

My Favorite John Ireland Westerns:

1. My Darling Clementine - **1946**

See the section on Henry Fonda for a complete description of this film. Ireland plays the pivotal role of Billy Clanton, who has an affair with Doc's girlfriend Chihuahua and ends up shooting her before she can reveal his identify. He and the rest of the Clantons are then gunned down by the Earps and Doc Holiday at the Gunfight.

2. *Gunfight at the OK Corral* - 1957

See the section on Burt Lancaster for a complete description of the movie. Ireland is again a member of the Ike Clanton gang but this time he plays Johnny Ringo instead of Billy Clanton. However, he meets the same fate as in the earlier film. By the way, Billy Clanton is played by a young Dennis Hopper in this version of the story.

3. *Red River* - 1948

In *Red River*, Ireland is not a villain but as Cherry Valance is the best friend of one of the two leads, Montgomery Clift as Matt Garth. At the very end of the film, he attempts to prevent John Wayne (Tom Dunston) from killing his adopted son. Ireland's future wife, Joanne Dru, has a key role in this film.

John Ireland's part was drastically reduced in its final form from what was originally intended, some say because both Ireland and the director, Howard Hawks, were competing for the affection of leading lady Joanne Dru. Hawks disputed that fact and said that instead, it was related to Ireland's drinking and also that he kept losing his hat and gun a lot. Oh well.

John Wayne and Joanne Dru in what is probably a publicity photo from Red River. It's hard to believe that any guy would be interested in her, isn't it?

4. *I Shot Jesse James* - 1949

John Ireland played the title role of Bob Ford, one of the two Ford brothers who shot and killed the famous outlaw, Jesse James.

While the law is still after him, Jesse James (Reed Hadley) lives quietly in a rented house in St. Joseph, Missouri, under the alias of Tom Howard. His wife Zee begs him to end his association with the Ford brothers, whom she considers to be nothing but trouble. Before they can leave on one "last" bank holdup, Bob learns that his childhood sweetheart, Cynthy Waters (Barbara Britton), now an actress, is in town, and he brushes aside all caution to see her. Cynthy is beginning to realize that she is a liability to her manager, Harry Kane (J. Edward Bromberg), because she will not leave Missouri. Meanwhile, John Kelley (Preston Foster) has come into her life. She pleads with Bob to become an honest man. Cynthy tries to get a pardon for Bob, but the best offer she can get is for a 20-year stretch in prison. Then, the Governor offers amnesty and a $10,000 reward to any member of the James gang betraying Jesse. When his chance comes on April 3, 1882, Bob shoots Jesse in the back, supposedly while he is adjusting a picture on the wall. He gets the amnesty he sought but the reward is cut to $500. He also loses the love and respect of Cynthy in the process.

Reed Hadley starred in the 1946 serial, *Zorro's Fighting Legion*, as the title character. But with his wonderful baritone voice, his main contribution may have been as a narrator of films, including many government films.

> Speaking of serials – not the breakfast variety – they were an important form of film entertainment from the 30s through the early 50s. By far, the most famous serials were the three *Flash Gordon* serials of 1936, 1938, and 1940, with Buster Crabbe. Kids would flock to the movie theaters on a Saturday afternoon to see a few chapters of a serial and a couple of Three Stooges shorts as much as the double feature film showing that day.

5. *Vengeance Valley* - 1951

Burt Lancaster usually played parts with a lot of depth to them, especially after *From Here to Eternity*. In fact other than *Vengeance Valley*, the only other film where he played a totally upright hero with very few flaws is *Gunfight at the OK Corral*.

Here he's the orphan kid that gets taken in by rancher Ray Collins who grows up and becomes foreman and companion to Robert Walker, Collins's real son. Walker is a spoiled kid and Lancaster is constantly cleaning up after him. If this sounds a lot like *Man from Laramie* to you, you are not alone.

Walker is coming home to both his wife, Joanne Dru, and another girl (Sally Forrest) that he has fathered a child with. Lancaster is caught taking hush money over to Forrest by her completely useless and no-good brothers, played by John Ireland and Hugh O'Brian. They come to the erroneous conclusion that Lancaster is the father. That's where the fun begins.

6. *Bushwackers* - 1951

Another role in which Ireland plays the hero rather than the heel. Confederate veteran Jeff Waring (Ireland) arrives in Independence, Missouri shortly after the Civil War, and vows never again to use a gun. He finds that rancher Artemus Taylor (Lon Chaney, Jr.), a complete tyrant, and his henchmen, Sam Tobin (Lawrence Tierney) and Cree (Jack Elam), are forcing out the settlers in order to claim their land for the incoming railroad. Brassy Myrna Dell (Norah Taylor) is on hand as Taylor's independent daughter, only slightly less meaner than her father, and Dorothy Malone is the pretty school teacher on the side of Ireland. Needless to say, Ireland's passive outlook on life changes before the end of the film.

> As father and daughter, Norah Taylor did not get along at all with Lon Chaney, Jr. She said he was pretty much always drunk on the set, really mean, and not very cooperative at all. That's too bad, because I always liked Chaney, especially in his most famous role as Lawrence Talbot in *The Wolfman* and its many sequels.

7. *Gunslinger* – 1956

And yet another film where John Ireland was not the villain. Oracle, Texas Marshal Scott Hood is murdered and his wife, Rose (Beverly Garland), takes his badge – literally - and sets out on a personal vendetta to find the killers. She has two weeks to serve as acting Marshal before the new marshal arrives to take over.

Meanwhile, the unscrupulous Erica Page (Allison Page), the saloon-mistress, is busy buying up local property because she has a tip the railroad is going to make Oracle a depot stop. The cowardly mayor warns her that the railroad may not come to Oracle, but Erica already has that base covered; after she makes payment on the land, she has her henchman, Jake Hayes, murder the seller and return it to her so she can buy some more land – nice lady! Erica is a businesswoman who believes in a fast return on investment. But, in order to get away cleanly, if the railroad does not come through, she sends Jake out-of-state to Tombstone to hire a gunslinger to come kill Rose. He brings back a hired gun, Cane Miro (John Ireland) who instead falls in love with his intended target. And that's where the villainous Ms. Page's plans begin to fall apart.

Ireland and Garland make a good team in this rather average western. The film was directed by Roger Corman, who is most famous for directing a ton of 1950's B-horror films such as *The Beast with a Million Eyes, It Conquered the World, The Wasp Woman, Attack of the Crab Monsters,* and *A Bucket of Blood,* then moving on to a bunch of higher budget Vincent Price horror films like *The Pit and the Pendulum, House of Usher, Premature Burial, Tower of London, X:The Man with the X-Ray Eyes,* and *The Raven.*

Summary

John Ireland was a handsome leading man/supporting actor who moved easily between westerns, World War II movies, and crime dramas. While he had a number of excellent roles and played in several excellent films such as *Red River, All the King's Men,* and *My Darling Clementine,* he just never quite made it as an A-list leading man. Still, he deserves to be remembered as a pretty good heel and, once in a while, as a hero.

4. Jack Elam – 1920-2003

In my mind, Jack Elam was kind of a poor man's John Ireland. Similar features, tall and lanky, dark hair, but not nearly as good looking. And unlike Ireland, Elam was almost always the heel, or if not that, the drunk. Again, like Ireland, he seemed to focus on westerns and also crime dramas. He certainly made a lot of movie and television appearances – 206, according to the International Movie Data Base – and was still appearing on TV in the 1990's when he was in his 70s.

Definitely, he was the kind of actor where – if you don't recognize his name – as soon as you see his picture, with one eye out of place – you say, oh yeah, Jack Elam.

Lots of good Jack Elam westerns, but my favorites were:

1. Rawhide
2. High Noon – yes, he was in this movie
3. Gunfight at the O.K. Corral

4. Vera Cruz
5. The Comancheros
6. The Far Country
7. The Man from Laramie
8. The Way West

Biography

"The heavy today is usually not my kind of guy. In the old days, Rory Calhoun was the hero because he was the hero and I was the heavy because I was the heavy—and nobody cared what my problem was. And I didn't either. I robbed the bank because I wanted the money. I've played all kinds of weirdoes but I've never done the quiet, sick type. I never had a problem—other than the fact I was just bad." In his own words Jack Elam, the man with the off-kilter eye, described the type of heavy that made him one of the top five screen heavies in a career that spanned nearly 50 years with his rich repertoire of bad guys, scoundrels, gangsters and loveable bumblers. (In fact, I am surprised he was not in *Blazing Saddles*!)

William Scott Elam was born November 13, 1920, in Miami, Arizona, a tiny mining community 100 miles from Phoenix, then grew up in Phoenix. His mother died when Jack was about two and he lived with various families who made him earn at least part of his keep. He remembered picking cotton at six. When Jack was nine he was reunited with his father, a building and loan appraiser who suffered from a serious eye ailment which made it difficult for him to work. He had Jack fill out forms for him at night.

When Jack was 12, he suffered the loss of vision in his left eye when he was involved in a fight at a Boy Scout meeting and was jabbed in the eye with a pencil by another boy. Elam had no control over his wandering eye, "It does whatever the hell it wants," Jack laughed. But the handicap became an asset when he later turned to movie work, not as the hero but as the villain, of course. And it played well in comic situations as well.

After high school, Jack moved to California and attended Santa Monica Junior College and Modesto Junior College where he met his future wife, Jean Hodgert. Married in 1937, they had two children, Scott and Jeri. Jack had a third child, Jacqueline, with his second wife, Margaret (Jenny) Jennison whom he married in 1961 after his first wife passed away. Exempt from WWII military service because of his eye, Jack worked as a civilian for the Navy in Culver City in a defense plant.

During his 20s and early 30s, Jack took a position as both auditor and manager of the famed Bel Air Hotel. When the Bel Air sold, Jack proved himself to be a 'Jack of all Trades' working as an accountant, purchasing agent, business manager and controller at Hopalong Cassidy Productions. Working as an auditor looking at numbers put a strain on Jack's good eye, so his eye doctor told him to find a new line of work. Because of his contacts in the motion picture business, he was able to help establish financing for three films (two of which were *High Lonesome* and *The Sundowners*, both made in 1950) in exchange for a small role in each.

Jack's big break came in 1950 filming *Rawhide* for director Henry Hathaway. With strong encouragement from star Tyrone Power, Jack played one of the nastiest, most sadistic villains ever on the screen. Power urged Darryl Zanuck to put Elam under contract, which resulted in a seven year contract at 20th Century Fox. Jack was off and running and never stopped being in huge demand until his last film ("Bonanza: Under Attack" for TV) in 1995. He was even in a musical, 1955's *Kismet*, with Howard Keel in the lead, playing a character called Hassan-Ben.(Sounds like a Three Stooges character – Hassan Ben Sober – sound it out.)

Jack's career falls into three phases—in the '50s and '60s he was the meanest of screen heavies, that is, with the exception of being on the right side of the law as reformed gunfighter, J. D. Smith, deputy to Marshal Frank Ragan (Larry Ward) for 19 episodes of Warner Bros.' "The Dakotas" in 1963. When that series failed, WB put Jack into "Temple Houston" (1963-64) as Jeffrey Hunter's sidekick, George Taggart, another reformed gunfighter.

In the late '60s, beginning with *Support Your Local Sheriff* (1969) starring James Garner, Elam drifted into more comedic portrayals, often playing a self parodying western heavy such as Sam Urp on "F-Troop: Dirge of the Scourge" (1965). The star of "Gunsmoke", James Arness, said, "He (Jack) played a rogue kind of guy, but not a real mean heavy, although he could certainly do that. What made him distinctive was the fact he could play unusual characters and he had this marvelous face—it was one of a kind. Also he was a great card player, great at all kinds of gambling. He always took everybody's money when he was on the set. He was a wonderful guy."

Finally, when, as Elam put it, "I grew too old and too fat to jump on a horse," he grew a long beard and settled into loveable old coot characterizations on "Father Murphy", "Alias Smith and Jones", "Paradise" and in "Hawken's Breed", "Big Bad John", "Once Upon a Texas Train" and "Lucky Luke".

Pinned down as to his favorite film, it's *Support Your Local Gunfighter*. King Vidor and Burt Kennedy were directors Elam particularly admired. His work in "Ransom of Red Chief" led to a 1977 daytime Emmy nomination. In 1983 Jack received the Golden Boot Award and in 1994 he was inducted into the Cowboy Hall of Fame in Oklahoma City.

As Arness indicated, cards were always one of Jack's passions. An avid poker player and a proponent of Liar's Poker, the stories about Jack's gambling are legendary. For example, Jack was the only one who ever had in his contract at Warner Bros. (on "Temple Houston" and "Dakotas") the right to gamble on the set.

Will Hutchins (Sugarfoot on TV) summed up the Jack Elam he knew, "He was the brother I'd never had; my long-lost uncle who once blew into town with gifts and wild tales; my dad who died too soon. I liked Jack straight off, the way I liked his acting. The abiding intelligence and humanity of the man overwhelmed me. Today I see a lot of sensational actors on screen showing off, but where's the humanity? Jack Elam doesn't show off. He doesn't *show* you anything. He lets you discover it for yourself. Whether he plays the good bad guy or the bad good guy, he has the ability to take us along with him, so we seem to be working things out together."

Jack died at 82, October 20, 2003, of congestive heart failure at his home in Ashland, Oregon, where he'd lived since 1990.

Awards and Recognition

Jack Elam was nominated for a daytime Emmy award for his performance in "Ransom of Red Chief" in 1977. He received a Golden Boot Award in 1983.

Jack was inducted into the Hall of Great Western Performers of the National Cowboy and Western Heritage Museum in 1994, and rightly so.

My favorite Jack Elam westerns:

1. *Rawhide* – 1951

Vinnie Holt (Susan Hayward), a single woman traveling with her toddler niece, becomes stranded at Rawhide, a desert stagecoach stop managed by stationmaster Sam Todd (Edgar Buchanan) and his assistant Tom Owens (Tyrone Power). Owens is quickly impressed by Vinnie's independent self-confidence. Jim Zimmerman (Hugh Marlowe), a fugitive murderer from Huntsville Prison disguised as a deputy, plus three other ruthless escapees (Jack Elam as Tevis plus Dean Jagger and George Tobias) take over the station, intent on robbing the next day's gold shipment.

In one of his first significant roles, Jack cemented his reputation as a bad guy by threatening to shoot a baby to make it "dance," shooting hero Tyrone Power, and killing virtually everyone in the film except Tyrone Power and Susan Hayward. Mean and nasty Jack Elam in a typical role.

2. *High Noon* – 1952

High Noon has been previously discussed under the films of Gary Cooper and Katy Jurado. Jack Elam was a last-minute addition to the cast who plays a drunk that Marshal Gary Cooper lets out of jail just before the climatic gunfight. We then watch Elam mosey on over to the saloon.

Jack Elam mentioned what an honor it was to work with Gary Cooper and what a nice guy he was. I am not surprised.

3. *Gunfight at the O.K. Corral* – 1957

This film has also been previously reviewed under the films of Burt Lancaster and seems to be popping up quite a lot in this book! Jack Elam plays Tom McLowery, one of the members of the Clanton gang that goes up against the Earps and Doc Holiday at the O.K. Corral. It is interesting to note that both Jack Elam and John Ireland were in the film and both were members of the ill-fated Clanton gang.

4. *Vera Cruz* – 1954

Already reviewed under the films of Burt Lancaster. After the American Civil War, mercenaries travel to Mexico to fight in their revolution for money. The former soldier and gentleman Benjamin Trane (Gary Cooper) meets the gunman and killer Joe Erin (Burt Lancaster) and his men, one of whom is Jack Elam, and together they are hired by the Emperor Maximillian and the Marquis Henri de Labordere to escort the Countess Marie Duvarre to the harbor of Vera Cruz.

Ben and Erin find that the stagecoach is transporting US$ three million dollars in gold hidden below the seat and they scheme to steal it. Along their journey, betrayals and incidents happen changing their initial intentions. And Burt has that typical smile and grin that he displayed a lot in this film and others.

Another Lancaster photo. You just can never have too much of Burt Lancaster's smile and teeth in *Vera Cruz*.

5. *The Comancheros* – 1961

Texas Ranger Jake Cutter (John Wayne) arrests gambler Paul Regret (Stuart Whitman), but soon finds himself teamed with his prisoner in an undercover effort to defeat a band of renegade arms merchants and thieves who the Rangers have been trying to take out, known as Comancheros. They are led by Graile (Nehemiah Persoff). Jack Elam plays one of the Comancheros and is therefore a villain. Lee Marvin, Ina Balin, Bruce Cabot, Michael Ansara, and Edgar Buchanan co-star. Marvin plays a merchant who sells arms to the Comancheros, at least until he meets John Wayne.

This was the last big-screen performance of veteran western actor Guinn "Big Boy" Williams, who played in over 220 movies and television shows, mainly westerns. Big Boy was exactly that, 6'2" and mostly muscled Texan. Another one of those actors whose name you might not recognize, but you probably will recognize his face. He was in films like *The Alamo* with John Wayne, *Santa Fe Trail* and *Virginia City* with Errol Flynn, and *Billy the Kid* with Robert Taylor.[39]

---

[39] Robert Taylor is another one of those actors like Burt Lancaster and Gregory Peck who played in quite a few westerns.

GOOD GUYS, BAD GUYS, AND SIDEKICKS IN WESTERN MOVIES

6. *The Far Country* – 1954

One of the most entertaining of the Western movies to come out of the 1950s, this is a James Stewart vehicle in which he must take on the ruthlessness of the frontier. Set in the Yukon, Jeff Webster (Stewart) and his friends (including Walter Brennan and Jay C. Flippen) are driving cattle to market from Wyoming to Canada, where the boom towns pay top dollar for beef. When they arrive in Skagway, the corrupt sheriff of the town (John McIntire) steals the cattle and Stewart and Brennan are forced to fight for their herd. Together with the female saloon keeper of another town (Ruth Roman), they find themselves up against an evil they were not prepared for. When Brennan's character is killed, Jeff is forced to go up against the nasty sheriff. Good versus evil in incredible Yukon settings makes this an above average Western.

There are great performances from Roman as Rhonda Castle, the saloon owner, and Jack Elam as the sheriff's sloth-like deputy.

7. *The Man from Laramie* – 1955

This James Stewart western has already been discussed in the section on Stewart. In Anthony Mann's classic 1955 western, Jack Elam introduces his character as follows: "I can't give you any references, but anyone can tell you Chris Boldt is not a man to be trusted." Later on, he tries to stab James Stewart in the back but instead winds up dead in a dark alley.

8. *The Way West* - 1967

In the mid-19th century, Senator William J. Tadlock (Kirk Douglas) leads a group of settlers overland in a quest to start a new settlement in the Western US. Tadlock is a highly principled and demanding taskmaster who is as hard on himself as he is on those who have joined his wagon train. He clashes with one of the new settlers, Lije Evans (Richard Widmark), who doesn't quite appreciate Tadlock's ways. Along the way, the families must face death and heartbreak and a sampling of frontier justice when one of them accidentally kills a young Indian boy. Elam plays a well-oiled preacher who is part of the group of settlers.

Summary

Jack Elam was an old-fashioned western heel who also made his mark in crime dramas and television. He was much more than just that wandering eye, but it sure helped in playing villains. "I drank scotch and played poker." That's what Jack Elam always said he wanted on his tombstone.

5. Victor Jory – 1902-1982

Like most of the bad guys in this book, Victor Jory relished playing villains but was a nice guy in real life. His commanding presence and deep, resonant voice made him perfect as an in-charge heavy. His mesmerizing coal-black eyes could hold you in a trance when combined with his distinctive, fascinating clipped manner of speaking with dramatic pauses. Jory was a unique actor indeed whose career took on many facets over 50 years.

The following are my favorite Victor Jory westerns:

1. Gone with the Wind
2. The Man from the Alamo
3. Dodge City
4. Bad Men of Missouri
5. The Adventures of Tom Sawyer
6. Canadian Pacific

Biography

Victor Jory was born November 23, 1902, in Dawson City, Yukon Territory, Canada, the son of Edwin Jory, a horse trader who was a native of Oregon. Jory's mother was a native of Virginia who was one of the few working newspaperwomen in the Canadian wilderness. Actually, his parents were divorced before Vic was born. Born into a very poor environment, an uncle on his mother's side got him a job at $4 a day in a paper mill in Astoria, Oregon.

While working at the Hammond Lumber Company Jory accidentally received a deadly electrical shock from a huge electrical turbine that generated power for 18 surrounding towns. Doctors, concerned he might lose the use of his left arm, advised him to take up boxing. With no place in Astoria where he could learn to box, the now-14 year old Jory moved to Vancouver, British Columbia, where his mother owned some property. Learning boxing, he soon defeated four opponents to become the cruiser-weight golden gloves champion of that province. From age 14 to 17 he spent a good amount of time in the ring, earning from $7.50 to $15 a bout.

When he also found he could earn an extra one dollar by doing "Walk on" bits at Vancouver's Empress Theatre, he became interested in acting. Turning 18, he attended the Pasadena Community Playhouse – a training ground for many young actors and actresses - and attended the University of California for a semester. Vic then began a 10 year theatrical apprenticeship that included work in various stock companies across the U.S. Jory eventually made his Broadway debut in 1929 in "Berkeley Square" with Leslie Howard.

Jory was playing the lead in the Norman Krasna comedy "Louder, Please" in California when he was approached by a Fox talent scout. His first film was *Renegades* in 1930 with Warner Baxter.

On December 23, 1928, Jory married actress Jean Inness. They appeared on stage a number of times over the years. Inness made many films *("Gun Fever", "The Gunfighter", "Rosemary's Baby")* and TV episodes ("Big Valley', "Gunsmoke", "Peter Gunn", "Rawhide", "Twilight Zone", "Virginian: Return of Golden Tom" with her husband, "Dragnet", etc.) as well as directing 31 plays at the Pasadena Playhouse. Born December 18, 1900, Inness died December 27, 1978. The Jorys had two children, a son Jon who became the director of the Actors Theatre of Louisville, Kentucky, and a daughter Jean Jory Anderson, a public relations director of the theatre department at Utah State University.

Jory began playing villains in earnest in the 1930s. This included an early role as Injun Joe, one of the meanest, most brutish villains the movies ever gave us pursuing Tommy Kelly and Ann Gillis in *The Adventures of Tom Sawyer* (1938). Although he made many good films that year, 1939 was really a banner year for Jory, the year he "arrived". Among his 10 films that year were the gangster classic *Each Dawn I Die*, Shirley Temple's *Susannah of the Mounties*, his first big western *Dodge City* and of course as the carpetbagger overseer in *Gone With the Wind*.

Oddly enough, after these prestigious pictures, the next year, 1940, saw him playing the lead in two Columbia serials (Lamont Cranston as *The Shadow* and *The Green Archer*)[40] and joining the ranks of producer Harry "Pop" Sherman's stock company in two medium-budget westerns (*Knights of the Range* and *Cherokee Strip*). Jory would eventually make 12 pictures for Sherman, including seven Hopalong Cassidy entries.

Jory continued his stage career even after he was in motion pictures. Jory co-starred on Broadway in "The Two Mrs. Carrolls." After the war, in 1945 Jory did "Therese" with Dame May Whitty and in 1946 was a member of the new American Repertory Theatre in New York.

World War II and Broadway gave Jory a four year break from the B-westerns he'd been doing, so when he returned to Hollywood in 1948 he began to be featured in bigger pictures once again. Dramatic television also became a part of his life in 1950 ("Philco Television Playhouse", "Studio One", "Broadway Television Theatre", for

---

[40] Another actor who was not afraid to appear in an occasional serial.

example.). In 1958 Vic filmed 78 episodes of the San Diego based "Dragnet"-like cop series, "Manhunt" co-starring Patrick McVey.

In '59, filmed in Milton, New York, Jory acted in what he termed his favorite role, that of a Mississippi general store owner who is dying of cancer and who is afraid of losing his no-good wife (Anna Magnani) to drifter Marlon Brando. *The Fugitive Kind*, was poorly received, however.

Jory took a filming break '60-'62 and returned that year to play Helen Keller's father in *The Miracle Worker*. He also began to work hard in episodic television. In 1964, now a craggy-faced 62, Jory played the part of Indian Chief Tall Tree in John Ford's homage to westerns, *Cheyenne Autumn*. The role opened up another facet of Jory's career as he began to play elderly Indians in other films (*Flap*, *Papillon*) and on TV ("Nakia", "Gunsmoke", "Virginian", "Young Maverick"). It was the role of a 109 year old Indian, Iron Belly, in *Mountain Men* that brought the end to Jory's illustrious career in 1980.

Jory died February 12, 1982, at 79, of a heart attack at his home in Santa Monica. He had had a long history of coronary trouble. On screen Jory played heavies with a great deal of enthusiasm, but in real life he was known by his broad smile, and calm, astute, charming manner.

My Favorite Victor Jory Westerns

1. *Gone with the Wind* – 1939

OK, it's not a western. But the 1939 classic about the Civil War and Reconstruction from the point of view of the South is perhaps the most famous film in American history. While Jory has a small part, it is an important one. He plays Jonas Wilkerson, a "poor white trash" farmer before the war who becomes a carpetbagger after the war in order to take advantage of those who were devastated by the war.

Victor Jory in *Gone with the Wind*

2. *The Man from the Alamo* - 1953

Already covered under Glenn Ford. During the war for Texas independence, one man leaves the Alamo before the end (chosen by lot to help others' families) but is too late to accomplish his mission, and is branded a coward. Since he cannot now expose a gang of turncoats, he infiltrates them instead. Can he save a wagon train of settlers moving West – mainly women - from Wade's Guerillas? Jory plays Wade, a mean and nasty guy, who wants to kill them and steal all their possessions. Ford and Chill Wills are the two remaining men, but the females – including Julie Adams - more than help the good guys in this pretty good western.

3. *Dodge City* – 1939

Errol Flynn actually made some pretty good westerns, English accent and all – *They Died with Their Boots on*, *San Antonio*, *Virginia City*, *Santa Fe Trail* – and this is one of the best of them. Dodge City is a wide-open cattle town run by Jeff Surrett (Bruce Cabot). Even going on a children's Sunday outing is not a safe thing to do. What the place needs is a fearless honest Marshal, perhaps Wade Hatton (Flynn), who helped bring the railroad to Dodge City. It may not help that he fancies Abbie Irving (Olivia de Haviland), who won't have anything to do with him since he had to shoot her brother. Jory plays Yancey, naturally a no-good-nick and one of Surrett's henchmen.

Errol Flynn and Olivia de Haviland made eight films together, including *Captain Blood* and my personal favorite – *The Adventures of Robin Hood* – pictured above. Born in 1916, as of the writing of this book, she is still alive.

4. *Bad Men of Missouri* - 1941

I always like films about Jesse James, and this was another one involving the James/Younger brothers partnership. The Younger brothers, Cole (Dennis Morgan), Bob (Wayne Morris) and Jim (Arthur Kennedy), return to Missouri after the Civil War with intent to avenge the misdeeds of William Merrick (Victor Jory), a crooked banker who has been buying up warrants on unpaid back-taxes and dispossessing the farmers. Henry Younger (Russell Simpson), their father, has been killed by a Merrick henchman and then Cole is framed on a murder rap. The brothers escape and then begin a series of bank and train robberies with Jesse James (Alan Baxter), primarily stealing from Merrick and turning the loot over to the farmers. Jim, in love with Mary Hathaway (Jane Wyman), is lured into Harrisonville and jailed. Jory plays his usual mean and despicable self.

Alan Baxter played lots of white-collar villains and killers in the 30s and 40s. My favorite Alan Baxter film is Alfred Hitchcock's *Saboteur*, where he played a Nazi spy living in the US, talking about his kids and their school activities – ironic.

5. *The Adventures of Tom Sawyer* - 1938

This 1938 film version of the classic Mark Twain novel starring Tommy Kelly as Tom Sawyer and Jackie Moran as Huck Finn includes most of the sequences familiar to readers of the book, including the fence-whitewashing episode; a wild raft ride down the Mississippi River; Tom and Huckleberry Finn's attendance at their own funeral, (after the boys, who were enjoying an adventure on a remote island, are presumed dead); the murder trial of local drunkard Muff Potter (Walter Brennan); and Tom and Becky Thatcher's flight through a cave as they try to escape from Injun Joe, who is revealed to be the real killer.

Victor Jory is superbly cast as Injun Joe. Because of his dark complexion, swarthy looks, and menacingly deep voice, he is perfect as the villain in this film.

6. *Canadian Pacific* - 1949

After finding a vital pass through the Canadian Rockies for the building of the Canadian Pacific Railway, Tom Andrews (Randolph Scott) tells his boss Cornelius Van Horne (Robert Barrat) that he is resigning to marry the girl he loves, Cecille Gautier (Nancy Olson). From Cecille, Tom learns that fur trader Dirk Rourke (Victor Jory) fears the coming of the railroad because it threatens his hold on the Indians and other trappers. Tom and Rourke have a bitter fight over Cecille, and Tom asks her to wait for him, as he has to go back and finish his job with the railroad. Aided by Dynamite Dawson (J.Carrol Naish), Tom finds evidence of Rourke's work against the railroad construction and almost loses his life when Rourke fires into some crates of dynamite Tom is unloading. The construction camp's doctor, Edith Cabot (Jane Wyatt), gives her own blood in a transfusion to save Tom's life. Additional complications arise.

Another western in which Victory Jory is a menacingly effective villain.

Summary

Victor Jory could and did play everything from Irish men to Native Americans. And while he made lots of films that were not westerns, he was particularly good in the western genre. With his dark, swarthy features, menacing look, and low voice, he was a natural villain. Another guy who off screen was a really good guy. That's why they call it acting, I guess.

6. Arthur Kennedy – 1914-1990

One of my favorite actors of the 1940s through 1960s, Arthur Kennedy was one of the few guys who could play leading men and heels with equal aplomb. While he was a villain in many westerns and crime dramas, he was the newspaper reporter/narrator in *Lawrence of Arabia* and Kirk Douglas's good-guy brother in *Champion*. An accomplished stage actor, he played Biff in "Death of a Salesman" and several other plays on Broadway before moving to Hollywood full time in the early 1940s to work mainly in films after that. An actor's actor, he was nominated for Oscars five times but never won one.

There are a lot of good Arthur Kennedy westerns out there, but these are my favorites:

1. Bend of the River
2. The Man from Laramie
3. Day of the Evil Gun
4. They Died with Their Boots On

5. Bad Men of Missouri
6. The Lusty Men
7. Cheyenne Autumn

Biography

Born John Arthur Kennedy (I guess there were already enough John Kennedys around, for him to go by Arthur instead of John) to a dentist and his wife on February 17, 1914 in Worcester, Massachusetts. As a young man, known as "Johnny" to his friends, Kennedy studied drama at the Carnegie Institute of Technology. By the time he was 20 years old, he was involved in local theatrical groups. Kennedy's first professional gig was with the Globe Theatre Company, which toured the Midwest offering abbreviated versions of Shakespearian plays. Famed actor Maurice Evans hired Kennedy for his company, with which he appeared in the Broadway production of "Richard II" in 1937. While performing in Evans' repertory company, Kennedy also worked in the Federal Theatre Project.[41]

Arthur Kennedy made his Broadway debut in "Everywhere I Roam" in 1938, the same year that he married Mary Cheffrey, who would remain his wife until her death in 1975. He also appeared on Broadway in "Life and Death of an American" in 1939 and in "An International Incident" in 1940 at the Ethel Barrymore Theatre.

---

[41] The Federal Theater Project was a New Deal program administered by the Works Progress Administration that was designed to fund theatre and other live artistic performances and entertainment programs in the United States during the Great Depression. It was created not as a cultural activity but as a relief measure to employ artists, writers, directors and theater workers. It was shaped into a federation of regional theatres that created relevant art, encouraged experimentation in new forms and techniques, and made it possible for millions of Americans to see live theatre for the first time. The Federal Theatre Project ended when its funding was canceled after strong Congressional objections to the left-wing political tone of a small percentage of its productions.

Kennedy and his wife moved west to Los Angeles, California in 1938, and it was while acting on the stage in L.A. that he was discovered by fellow Irish-American actor James Cagney, who cast him as his brother in the film *City for Conquest* (1940). The role brought with it a contract with Warner Bros., and the studio put him in supporting roles in some prestigious movies, including *High Sierra* (1941), the film that made Humphrey Bogart a star, *They Died with Their Boots On* (1941) with Errol Flynn, and Howard Hawks' *Air Force* (1943) alongside future Best Supporting Actor Oscar winner Gig Young and John Garfield. His career was interrupted by military service in World War Two.

After the war, Kennedy went back to the Broadway stage, where he gained a reputation as an actor's actor, appearing in Arthur Miller's 1947 Tony Award-winning play "All My Sons," which was directed by Elia Kazan. He played John Proctor in the original production of Miller's reflection on McCarthyism, "The Crucible" - which Kazan, an informer who cooperated with the forces of McCarthyism, refused to direct - and also appeared in Miller's last Broadway triumph, "The Price."

When Kennedy returned to film work, he quickly distinguished himself as one of the best and most talented of supporting actors & character leads, appearing in such major films as *Boomerang!* (1947), *Champion* (1949) (for which he received his first Oscar nomination as Best Supporting Actor) and *The Glass Menagerie* (1950), playing Tom in a decent adaptation of Tennessee Williams classic play. Kennedy won his first and only Best Actor nomination for *Bright Victory* (1951), playing a blinded vet, a role for which he won the New York Film Critics Circle award over such competition as Marlon Brando and Humphrey Bogart. Other films included Fritz Lang's *Rancho Notorious* (1951), Anthony Mann's *Bend of the River* (1952), William Wyler's *The Desperate Hours* (1955), Richard Brooks' *Elmer Gantry* (1960), David Lean's *Lawrence of Arabia* (1962), and John Ford's *Cheyenne Autumn* (1964).

In 1956, Kennedy won another Best Supporting Actor Oscar nomination for his role in *Trial* (1955), plus two more Supporting nods in 1958 and 1959 for his appearances in the screen adaptations of Grace Metalious' *Peyton Place* (1957), and James Jones' *Some Came Running* (1958).

Kennedy returned to Broadway frequently in the 1950s, and headlined the 1952 play "See the Jaguar," a flop best remembered for giving a young actor named James Dean one of his first important parts. A decade later, Kennedy replaced his good friend Anthony Quinn in the Broadway production of "Beckett", alternating the roles of Beckett and Henry II with Laurence Olivier, who was quite fond of working with Kennedy. In the 1960s, the prestigious movie parts dried up as he matured, but he continued working in movies and on TV until he retired in the mid-1980s. Never remarrying after the passing of his wife, he moved out of Los Angeles to live with family members in Connecticut. In the last years of his life, he was afflicted with thyroid cancer and eye disease. He died of a brain tumor at 75, survived by his two children, Terence and actress Laurie Kennedy. He is buried at Woodlawn Cemetery in Lequille, Nova Scotia, Canada.

Awards and Recognition

Because he was an accomplished actor, he probably got better parts to choose from than some of the other supporting actors/villains on this list.

As a result, Arthur Kennedy was nominated for five Oscars but did not win any. They were as follows:

1950 – Best Actor in a Supporting Role – *Champion*

1952 – Best Actor in a Leading Role – *Bright Victory*

1956 – Best Actor in a Supporting Role – *Trial*

1958 – Best Actor in a Supporting Role – *Peyton Place*

1959 – Best Actor in a Supporting Role – *Some Came Running*

He was nominated for two Golden Globe awards and won one:

1952 – Best Actor in a Drama – *Bright Victory*

1956 – Best Supporting Actor – *Trial* – won the Golden Globe

He also won Laurel awards for second place for *A Summer Place* (1960), *Some Came Running* (1958), and *Peyton Place* (1957)

My Favorite Arthur Kennedy Westerns

1. *Bend of the River* - 1952

Already covered under the films of James Stewart. Two buddies with questionable pasts, Glyn McLyntock (Stewart) and his friend Cole, (Arthur Kennedy) lead a wagon-train load of homesteaders from Missouri to the Oregon territory. They establish a settlement outside Portland and as winter nears, it is necessary for them to rescue and then deliver food and supplies being held in Portland by corrupt officials. On the trip back to the settlement, up river and over a mountain, Cole engineers a mutiny to divert the supplies to a gold mining camp for a handsome profit. Kennedy is terrific moving from buddy to baddy.

Kennedy and Stewart are good buddies through about 2/3 of the film when Kennedy suddenly turns the tables and becomes a vicious killer. That does not impress his fiancé (Julie Adams) at all, nor Rock Hudson in an early role. Beautiful in Technicolor and a very underrated western.

2. *The Man from Laramie* - 1955

Already covered under the films of James Stewart, this movie is just as good, if not better, than *Bend of the River*. And another case where Arthur Kennedy's character is a seemingly good guy who is not quite what he seems and is eventually pitted against Stewart's character. The film features good performances by Donald Crisp as rancher Alec Waggoman and Alex Nicol as his vicious, irresponsible son, who supplements his income by illegally selling rifles to the nearby Apache Indians, as well as the aforementioned Cathy O'Donnell as the love interest.

3. *Day of the Evil Gun* - 1968

Another "buddy" movie with an uneasy relationship, this time featuring an older Glenn Ford and Arthur Kennedy. Gunfighter Lorn Warfield (Ford) returns home after an absence of three years and finds his ranch in ruins. His neighbor, Owen Forbes (Kennedy), informs Lorn that his ranch was raided by the Apaches, who kidnapped his wife and two children.

Lorn then decides to find the Apache camp and recapture his wife and daughters. Owen also joins Lorn in his quest. The two men don't get along because Owen courted Lorn's wife in Lorn's absence. Angie (Barbara Babcock) consented to Owen's courtship only because she believed her husband Lorn to be dead.

Despite the tension between Lorn and Owen, the two men are determined to find Angie and her daughters. Things get really hard when Lorn and Owen run into a series of obstacles including Mexican bandits, army deserters and Apaches.

4. *They Died with Their Boots on* – 1941

As stated earlier, Errol Flynn actually made a number of quality westerns, and this was one of them, the highly inaccurate story of General George Armstrong Custer, who was killed at the Battle of The Little Big Horn in 1876 by the Sioux Indians.

Custer has little discipline early on at West Point but is prepared to stand up to the senior cadet, Ned Sharp (Arthur Kennedy), who makes his life miserable.

GOOD GUYS, BAD GUYS, AND SIDEKICKS IN WESTERN MOVIES

Errol Flynn and Arthur Kennedy, among others, in an early scene from *They Died with Their Boots On*.

> For a fellow from Tasmania, Errol Flynn certainly made a number of quality westerns. Those included, in addition to *They Died with Their Boots On*, *San Antonio*, *Dodge City*, *Virginia City*, and *Santa Fe Trail*.

5. *Bad Men of Missouri* – 1941

Already covered under the films of Victor Jory. Arthur Kennedy plays one of the Younger Brothers, who frequently teamed up with the James brothers to rob banks and create other mischief after the Civil War.

6. *The Lusty Men* – 1952

This 1952 film featured an excellent cast that included Robert Mitchum and Susan Hayward. When he sustains a rodeo injury, star rider Jeff McCloud (Mitchum) returns to his hometown after many years of absence. He signs on as a hired hand with a local ranch, where he befriends fellow ranch hand Wes Merritt (Kennedy) and his wife Louise (Hayward). Wes has big dreams of owning his own farm, and rodeo winnings could help finance it. Wes convinces Jeff to coach him in the rodeo ways, but Louise has her doubts. She doesn't want her man to end up a broken down rodeo bum like Jeff McCloud. Despite Louise's concern, the threesome hit the road in pursuit of Wes' dream, chucking a secure present for an unknown future.

7. *Cheyenne Autumn* - 1964

Cheyenne Autumn is a 1964 Western movie starring Richard Widmark, Carroll Baker, James Stewart, and Edward G. Robinson, among others. Regarded as an epic film, it tells the story of a factual event, the Northern Cheyenne Exodus of 1878-9, although it is told in 'Hollywood style' using a great deal of artistic license. The film was the last Western directed by John Ford, who proclaimed it a tribute to the Native Americans who had been abused by the U.S. government and misrepresented by many of the director's own films. With a budget of more than $4,000,000, the film was relatively unsuccessful at the box office.

The original version was 158 minutes, Ford's longest work. Warner Bros. later decided to edit the "Dodge City" sequence out of the film, reducing the running time to 145 minutes, although it was shown in theaters during the film's initial release. This sequence features James Stewart as Wyatt Earp, and Kennedy as Doc Holliday. Some critics have argued that this comic episode, mostly unrelated to the rest of an otherwise serious movie, breaks the flow of the story. However, it was later restored for the VHS and subsequent DVD releases.

Summary

In addition to his film career, Arthur Kennedy was an outstanding stage actor, appearing in many top-quality plays on Broadway. In films, he alternated between playing the hero and the villain, including playing both in some movies. And whatever he did, he did it well, as evidenced by his five Oscar nominations.

7. John Carradine – 1906-1988

Probably known more for his roles in horror films than anything else, tall and gaunt-looking John Carradine also played in many westerns along the way, generally as the villain. A protégé and close friend of John Barrymore, Carradine not surprisingly also simultaneously maintained a stage career in classic leading roles such as Hamlet and Malvolio. With his wonderful baritone voice, one can easily see him portraying Hamlet during a break from playing a mad scientist or monster – he played Dracula three times, including *House of Frankenstein* and *House of Dracula* – on the silver screen.

Carradine appeared in some really outstanding films, including *Stagecoach*, *The Grapes of Wrath*, *The Bride of Frankenstein*, *The Ten Commandments*, *Jesse James*, and *Drums Along the Mohawk*, just to name a few.

Carradine, whose acting career spanned more than a half-century, was the patriarch of an American acting family. Four of his five sons, David, Robert, Keith and Bruce, have acted in movies and on television. Only Christopher Carradine chose not to follow in his father's footsteps; he became an architect, probably a nobler profession.

My favorite John Carradine films were mostly horror films, where he tended to play lead roles. But my favorite John Carradine westerns were the following:

1. Stagecoach
2. Drums Along the Mohawk
3. Jessie James
4. The Return of Frank James
5. The Kentuckian
6. The Man Who Shot Liberty Valance

Biography

Richmond Reed Carradine, the son of a reporter/artist and a surgeon, was born on February 5, 1906 in Greenwich Village in New York City and grew up in Poughkeepsie, New York. He attended Christ Church School and Graphic Art School, studying sculpture and art.

Carradine hitchhiked around the South for a time, sketching local businessmen and their daughters. "If the sitter was satisfied, the price was $2.50," he once said. "It cost him nothing if he thought it was a turkey. I made as high as $10 to $15 a day." (Probably decent money in the 1920s.)

But John got interested in acting, and in 1925 he won a featured role in a New Orleans production of "Camille." He then joined a touring Shakespearean stock company, winding up in 1927 in Hollywood, where he earned a lean living in local stage productions. At that time, he applied for a job as a scenic designer to Cecil B. DeMille, who rejected his designs but gave him voice work in several films. His on-screen debut was in *Tol'able David* (1930).

Tall and gaunt and possessing a deep and mellow baritone voice, Carradine early impressed critics and audiences alike with his first important movie role, as Preacher Casy in John Ford's *Grapes of Wrath*.

In private life, he amusedly cultivated a reputation as an eccentric and a bit of a ham – you can tell that from watching his horror films, where he occasionally overacted. Dressed in a red-lined satin cape and wearing a wide-brimmed hat, he liked to stroll the streets of Los Angeles and New York while reciting Shakespearean dialogue. Perhaps as a result, in Hollywood he was sometimes called the "Bard of the Boulevard."

He often toured as Hamlet in the 1940's, but his Broadway appearances were becoming fewer and fewer. Carradine's last major role in New York was in the 1962 musical comedy "A Funny Thing Happened on the Way to the Forum," in which he played Lycus, a likeable dealer in courtesans.

As a member of director John Ford's informal "stock company" of character actors, which included Ward Bond, Wallace Ford, Jane Darwell and Walter Brennan, Carradine appeared in ten Ford films. These included *The Prisoner of Shark Island* (1936), in which he was the sadistic guard of Dr. Samuel Mudd. Other Ford films in which Carradine appeared included *Mary of Scotland* (1936), *The Hurricane* (1937), *Drums Along the Mohawk* (1939), *Stagecoach* (1939), *The Last Hurrah* (1958), *The Man Who Shot Liberty Valance* (1962) and *Cheyenne Autumn* (1964).

Carradine, who changed his name to John Carradine in 1935, is probably best known today for the dozens of B movies, typically in the horror genre, as mad doctors, demented scientists and sadistic criminals. He played the bloodthirsty vampire Dracula in three movies, including the beguilingly titled *Billy the Kid vs. Dracula*,' in 1966.

Like his friend Vincent Price, who played similar roles, he was not above hamming and mugging for the camera.

> *House of Dracula* – 1945 – was noteworthy for being the film in which the wolfman - Larry Talbot - (Lon Chaney, Jr.) is finally cured of being the wolfman, and he even gets the girl, the very beautiful Martha O'Driscoll.

Carradine said that among his favorite movies were *Of Human Hearts* (1938), in which he played Lincoln; *Hitler's Madman* (1943), in which he appeared as the Nazi general Reinhard Heydrich; *The Adventures of Mark Twain* (1944), in which he was seen as the writer Bret Harte, and DeMille's *Ten Commandments* (1956), in which he played Aaron.

"I never made big money in Hollywood," Mr. Carradine said in 1986. "I was paid in hundreds, the stars got thousands. But I worked with some of the greatest directors in films, and some of the greatest writers. They gave me freedom to do what I can do best and that was gratifying."

Whenever he could, he returned to his beloved Shakespearean roles, usually on tours. In 1952 he included some Shakespeare, along with passages from Shaw, Rupert Brooke and the Bible, in a one-man recital at the Village Vanguard, a nightclub in Greenwich Village.

He said he often advised his actor sons: "Read all the Shakespeare you can. If you play Shakespeare, you can play anything."

John Carradine died at age 82 of natural causes on November 27, 1988. He was married and divorced three times. With around 350 film and television credits, John Carradine was certainly a busy fellow.

Awards

Among his awards, John Carradine was nominated for a Daytime Emmy award in 1985 for his performance in a children's program, "Umbrella Jack." He was also the recipient of a Golden Boot award in 1984 as a distinguished performer in western films.

My Favorite John Carradine Westerns

1. *Stagecoach* – 1939

This is the western that made John Wayne a star, taking him from low-budget films and serials and placing at the top of the A list of movie stars of that era.

In 1855, the Overland stage from Tonto to Lordsburg leaves town with eight people on board. In the front, sit Buck the driver (Andy Devine) and Marshal Curley Wilcox (George Bancroft), who is riding shotgun to protect the stage from hostile Indians and from the Plummer brothers, a vicious band of outlaws. The passengers consist of Doc Josiah Boone, the town drunk (Thomas Mitchell); Dallas (Claire Trevor), a woman of ill repute, who, like Doc, has been banished from town; the pregnant Lucy Mallory (Louise Platt), who is taking the stage to meet her husband, a cavalry officer, and is treated gallantly by her fellow passenger, Hatfield (John Carradine), a gambler; Gatewood (Berton Churchill), the town's sanctimonious banker who mouths respectability while clutching a carpet bag filled with stolen money from his bank; and Peacock (Donald Meek), a timid whiskey drummer. Because of an Apache uprising by Geronimo, the cavalry escorts the coach to the first station at Dry Fork.

Along the way, Buck stops to pick up the Ringo Kid (John Wayne), who has escaped from prison to seek revenge on the Plummers, who killed his family and sent him to jail on false testimony. After Curley arrests Ringo, the stage continues on to Dry Fork, where they discover that there are no troops to escort them farther. Voting to continue on alone, they reach the next stop, where their journey is delayed when Mrs. Mallory, learning that her husband has been wounded, goes into premature labor. Doc sobers up to deliver the baby, and as they await Mrs. Mallory's recovery, Dallas and Ringo fall in love and Dallas urges Ringo to escape. Ringo is on the verge of leaving when he sees Apache war signals, and the passengers hastily board the stage to make a desperate dash to Lordsburg. Further adventures await them as they make their way to Lordsburg as well as once they are in Lourdsburg.

This is simply one of the best westerns of all time, with a terrific ensemble cast and an exciting plot. John Carradine's character is very respectful of Mrs. Mallory, because she, like he, is a Southerner, but is very disdainful of Dallas because of her background.

> Perhaps there was no actor who was a better fit for his name than Donald Meek. Standing only 5'4" and bald, he was continuously playing nebbishes in films like *Stagecoach*, *State Fair*, and *You Can't Take It with You*. However, when he was young he was a member of an acrobatic team that toured the United States; He also fought in the Spanish American War and also saw action in World War I. So go figure.

The appropriately-named Donald Meek.

2. *Drums Along the Mohawk* – 1939

Already covered under the films of Henry Fonda. *Drums Along the Mohawk* is a 1939 historical Technicolor film based upon a 1936 novel of the same name by American author, Walter D. Edmonds. The film was produced by Darryl F. Zanuck and directed by John Ford. Henry Fonda and Claudette Colbert portray settlers (Gilbert and Lana Martin) on the New York frontier during the American Revolution. The couple suffer British, Tory, and Indian attacks on their farm before the Revolution ends and peace is restored. The film—Ford's first color feature— was nominated for two Academy Awards and became a major box office success, grossing over $1 million in its first year, not bad for 1939.

Carradine plays Caldwell, a Tory who is leading raiding parties of Seneca Indians against the settlers. They destroy the Martins' farm, which causes them to accept work on the farm of a wealthy widow, Mrs. McKlennar (Edna Mae Oliver). As usual, Carradine is doing his dirty work and is pitted against the good guys, in this case the Martins.

3. *Jesse James* – 1939

The very fictionalized story of Jesse James (Tyrone Power) and then the sequel, in which his brother Frank (Henry Fonda in both movies) seeks to exact revenge against the two brothers – Bob and Charley Ford – who murder Jesse by shooting him in the back. Carradine plays Bob Ford in both this film and the sequel, *The Return of Frank James*

Power and Fonda

In *Jesse James*, It is the usual rather fictional take on the actual events in the life of the famous outlaw.[42] The railroads are squeezing farmers off their land. When a railroad agent kills their mother, Frank and Jesse James (Henry Fonda and Tyrone Power) take up robbing banks and trains. While the public regards them as heroes, the railroads and banks want them captured and killed. When Jesse retires his erstwhile friend Robert Ford – John Carradine - shoots him in the back to get the reward and a pardon.

In real life, Jesse James was a cold-blooded killer. There is also no evidence that he shared the money he made from robberies with those who were less fortunate – not exactly Robin Hood.

This man might look like an innocent choir boy, but Jesse James was a killer, not the hero we see in movies.

---

[42] For a more factual account of the life of Jesse James, it is probably best to read something like *Jesse James: The Life, Times, and Treacherous Death of the Most Infamous Outlaw of All Time* or one of the other books on perhaps America's most famous bank robber.

GOOD GUYS, BAD GUYS, AND SIDEKICKS IN WESTERN MOVIES

4. *The Return of Frank James* - 1940

Made one year after Jesse James. Frank James (Henry Fonda), the brother of Jesse James, has been laying low, living as a farmer and taking care of Clem (Jackie Cooper), the young son of one of the members of the James gang. When he gets word that Jesse was killed by Bob and Charlie Ford, he hopes that the law will deal with them. But when he learns that the railroad man whom he and Jesse terrorized contracted with the Fords to kill Jesse and helped them get off, he goes after them. Clem, whom he told to remain on the farm, goes with him and when it's impossible for him to do so, Frank has no choice but to let him tag along.

In order to cover their tracks they start telling people that Frank James is dead and that they saw it. Eleanor Stone (Gene Tierney), a female reporter who wants to make a name for herself, interviews Frank and there is a definite attraction between them. But eventually she learns who Frank is from the Pinkerton detective who is tracking them, but doesn't turn Frank in. Frank tries to stay incognito but when he learns that his farm hand, Pinky (Ernest Whitman), has been arrested as his accomplice and is about to be hung, he realizes he must take action. John Carradine recreates his role as Bob Ford and gets his just desserts at the end of the film.

Sorry, but I just had to put in another photo of one of favorite female movie stars of all time, Gene Tierney. Do most redeemed criminals end up with someone who looks like her?

5. *The Kentuckian* – 1955

Burt Lancaster makes his directorial debut with this superb, action-packed western. Featuring a poignant, unconventional screenplay by A.B. Guthrie, Jr., and a powerful performance by legendary actor Walter Matthau in his first screen role as the villain, *The Kentuckian* is an unforgettable western adventure of the highest caliber.

Big Eli Wakefield (Lancaster) and his young son, Little Eli (Donald MacDonald), are rugged Kentucky adventurers who long for an exciting life on the Texas frontier. They soon learn, however, that the greatest challenge to their progress lies not in the uncharted wilderness but in the people they meet along the way. Thrust into the midst of a bitter family feud, Eli confronts both the deadly rage of a madman (Matthau) and the love of a beautiful woman (Diana Lynn). But when he's lured into a brutal final showdown, Eli discovers that the only way to escape with his life is to stay true to his convictions, his honor and his dream.

John Carradine is a snake-oil salesman whom Wakefield encounters.

6. *The Man Who Shot Liberty Valance* – 1962

When Senator Ransom Stoddard (James Stewart) returns home to Shinbone for the funeral of Tom Doniphon (John Wayne), he recounts to a local newspaper editor the story behind his association with Doniphon. He had come to town many years before as a young lawyer just getting started in his profession. The stage was robbed on its way in by the local ruffian, Liberty Valance (a very mean Lee Marvin), and Stoddard has none of his possessions left except for a few law books. He gets a job in the kitchen at the Ericson's restaurant and there meets his future wife, Hallie (Vera Miles).

The territory is vying for Statehood and Stoddard is selected as a representative over Valance, who continues terrorizing the town. When he destroys the local newspaper office and attacks the editor – Peabody - (Edmond O'Brien), Stoddard calls him out to fight, though the conclusion is not quite as straightforward as legend would have it.

At the statehood convention, Peabody nominates Stoddard as the territory's delegate to Washington, but his "unstatesmanlike" conduct is challenged by a rival candidate, Maj. Cassius Starbuckle (John Carradine, hamming it up). Stoddard decides that his opponent is right; he cannot be entrusted with public service after killing a man in a gunfight. But John Wayne (Doniphon) convinces him otherwise and lets him know who really shot Liberty Valance.

A great supporting cast includes Woody Strode as John Wayne's friend, and Jeanette Nolan and John Qualen as the Ericsons.

Woody Strode was a top athlete – football and decathlon – at UCLA and a good actor. At 6'4" and chiseled, he might have been a bigger star if he was born in 1974 instead of 1914. You might remember him for his fight to the death against Kirk Douglas in *Spartacus*. After he refuses to kill Spartacus, Strode is murdered by the Roman general – played by Lawrence Olivier. This leads to the slave revolt that almost brought Rome

to its knees. Strode was both African American and Native American. He died in 1994 at age 80. He was nominated for a Golden Globe for his performance in *Spartacus*, and served in the military in World War II.

Summary

With his beautiful mellow voice, John Carradine was a classically trained stage actor who made the transition to Hollywood with ease, typically playing villains in westerns and of course horror films. While his main claim to fame was mad scientists, mad doctors, and monsters, he also was outstanding in many western films. A ham on stage and on the set, he had four out of five sons, including David and Keith, who themselves opted for a career in acting.

8. Charles Bickford – 1891-1967

A character actor of wide ranging abilities and film types, gruff-voiced, gravelly-throated Charles Bickford was nominated for three Oscars as Best Supporting Actor in three different quality films – *The Song of Bernadette*, *The Farmer's Daughter*, and *Johnny Belinda*. Burly and brusque, he played heavies and father figures with equal skill. Bickford continued to act in generally prestigious films up until his death in 1967. While not specializing in westerns, he nonetheless made a number of quality western films throughout his long career.

Though Charles Bickford made a lot more films than just westerns, these are my favorite Bickford westerns:

1. The Big Country
2. The Unforgiven
3. A Big Hand for the Little Lady
4. The Plainsman
5. Duel in the Sun

Biography

Bickford was born in Cambridge, Massachusetts on January 1, 1891. The fifth of seven children, Charles was an intelligent but very independent and unruly child. For example, at the age of nine he was tried and acquitted of the attempted murder of a trolley motorman who had purposely driven over and killed his beloved dog. Charles was generally considered "the wild rogue" of this family, causing his parents frequent consternation. In his late teens he drifted aimlessly around the United States for a time, and in the process worked as a lumberjack, investment promoter, and for a short time, ran a pest extermination business.

Bickford had intended to attend the Massachusetts Institute of Technology to earn an engineering degree, but while wandering around the country, he became friends with the manager of a burlesque show[43], who convinced Bickford to take a role in the show. He debuted in Oakland, California in 1911. Bickford enjoyed himself so much that he abandoned his plans to attend M.I.T. He made his legitimate stage debut with the John Craig Stock Company at the Castle Square Theatre in Boston in 1912. He eventually joined a road company and traveled throughout the United States for more than a decade, appearing in various productions.

In 1925, while working in a Broadway play called "Outside Looking In," he and co-star James Cagney (in his first Broadway role) received rave reviews. Bickford was offered a role in Herbert Brenon's 1926 silent film version of *Beau Geste*, but anxious not to give up his newfound Broadway stardom, Bickford turned it down, a decision he later came to regret. Following his appearance in the critically praised but unsuccessful Maxwell Anderson-Harold Hickerson drama about the Sacco and Vanzetti case, "Gods of the Lightning" (Bickford was the Sacco character), Bickford was contacted by filmmaker Cecil B.

---

[43] Burlesque is a literary, dramatic or musical work intended to cause laughter by caricaturing the manner or spirit of serious works, or by ludicrous treatment of their subjects. The word derives from the Italian *burlesco*, which, in turn, is derived from the Italian *burla* – a joke, ridicule or mockery. It was especially popular during the 1920s.

DeMille and offered a contract with MGM studios to star in DeMille's first talking picture, *Dynamite*. He soon began working with MGM head Louis B. Mayer on a number of projects.

Charles soon became a star after playing Greta Garbo's lover in *Anna Christie* (1930), but for some reason never developed into a leading man. Always of independent mind, exceptionally strong-willed and quick with his fists, Bickford would frequently argue and nearly come to blows with Mayer and any number of other MGM authority figures during the course of this contract with the studio. During the production of DeMille's *Dynamite*, for example, he punched out his director following a string of heated arguments primarily related to the interpretation of his character's role. Throughout his early career on both the stage and later films, Bickford rejected numerous scripts and made no secret of his disdain for much of the material he was offered. Not surprisingly, his association with MGM and Mayer was short-lived with Bickford asking for and quickly receiving a release from his contract.

However, he soon found himself blacklisted at other studios forcing him to take the highly unusual step (common today but rare for that era) of becoming an independent actor for several years. His career took another turn when in 1935 he was mauled by a lion and nearly killed while filming *East of Java*. While he recovered, he lost his contract with Fox as well as his leading man status due to extensive neck scarring suffered in the attack coupled with his advancing age – now 44.

It was not long, however, before he made a very successful transition to character roles which he felt offered much greater diversity and allowed him to showcase his talent to better effect. Much preferring the character roles that now became his forte, Bickford appeared in many notable films including *The Farmer's Daughter*, *Johnny Belinda*, *A Star is Born*, and *Not As a Stranger*.

As a result of this career change, the once-difficult Charles Bickford quickly became highly sought after; his burly frame and craggy, intense features, coupled with a gruff, powerful voice lent themselves to a wide variety of roles. Most often he played lovable father figures, stern businessmen, heavies, ship captains, or authority figures of some sort, including westerns. During the 1940s, he was nominated three times for the Academy Award for Best Supporting Actor.

Bickford made a successful transition to the smaller screen during the early 50s. For example, he served as host of the 1950s television series *The Man Behind the Badge*. And on April 16, 1958, Bickford appeared with Roger Smith in "The Daniel Barrister Story" on NBC's *Wagon Train*. Bickford continued to act in generally prestigious projects right up to his death. He guest-starred on ABC's *The Islanders* and on NBC's *The Barbara Stanwyck Show* and *The Eleventh Hour*. In his final years, Bickford played rancher John Grainger, owner of the Shiloh Ranch on NBC's *The Virginian* western series.

Two of the actor's most later memorable big-screen roles came in the western *The Big Country* (1958), as a wealthy and ruthless rancher, and in the drama *Days of Wine and Roses*, as the forlorn father of an alcoholic.

Bickford was married for 52 years and had two children. He died in Los Angeles of a blood infection at the age of 76, on November 9, 1967, just days after filming an episode of *The Virginian*.

An outstanding actor, Charles Bickford was nominated for three Academy Awards for Best Supporting Actor but never won:

- *The Song of Bernadette* – 1943
- *The Farmer's Daughter* – 1947
- *Johnny Belinda* – 1948

He also won a 3rd place Laurel Award for his performance in *Days of Wine and Roses* (1962) and won an award from the National Board of Review as Best Supporting Actor for his performance in *Not As a Stranger* (1955.)

My Favorite Charles Bickford westerns:

1. *The Big Country* – 1958

A big-budget, sprawling, long (almost three hours) western, I have already discussed this film under the films of Gregory Peck, who is the overall star of the film. A very rousing western with an all-star cast.

Bickford plays Major Henry Terrill, a wealthy rancher. When Peck's character (Jim McKay) arrives on the scene to marry the major's spoiled daughter (Carol Baker), he finds that the Major is involved in a ruthless civil war over watering rights for cattle, with a rough clan led by Rufus Hannassey (Burl Ives). The land in question is owned by Julie Maragon (Jean Simmons) and both Terrill and Hannassey want the land in question. While McKay attempts to resolve the issue peacefully, he is unsuccessful. The climactic scene is a fight to the finish between Terrill and Hannassey.

2. *The Unforgiven* – 1960

Not to be confused with the 1992 Oscar-winning film with the same name but a completely different plot, which is directed by and stars Clint Eastwood, this film has already been mentioned under the films of Burt Lancaster. Bickford plays the leader of a group of neighbors who want to give Audrey Hepburn – supposedly a Kiowa Indian girl who was taken from her tribe as a baby – back to her people to avoid any trouble for the town, while her brother – Burt Lancaster – refuses to give in. Bickford has a relatively small but important role as the spokesperson for the neighbors.

3. *A Big Hand for the Little Lady* – 1966

The five richest men in the territory gather in Laredo, Texas for their annual high-stakes poker game. The high rollers let nothing get in the way of their yearly showdown. When undertaker Tropp (Charles Bickford) calls for them in his horse-drawn hearse, cattleman Henry Drummond (Jason Robards) forces a postponement of his daughter's wedding, while lawyer Otto Habershaw (Kevin McCarthy) abandons his closing arguments in a trial, with his client's life hanging in the balance. They are joined by Wilcox (Robert Middleton), Buford (John Qualen) and Bickford in the back room of the local saloon, while the townspeople gather outside for occasional updates on the progress of the game.

Settler Meredith (Henry Fonda), his wife Mary (Joanne Woodward), and their young son Jackie (Gerald Michenaud) are passing through, on their way to purchase a farm near San Antonio, when a wheel on their wagon breaks. They wait at the saloon while the local blacksmith repairs it. Meredith, a recovering gambler, learns of the big poker game and begins to feel the excitement once again. During a break, Otto Habershaw catches a glimpse of Mary in her violet dress. Being so enchanted by her, he permits Meredith's request to watch the game only if Mary approves. But Meredith soon buys into the game, eventually staking all of the family savings, meant to pay for the farm.

The game builds to a climactic hand; the gamblers raise and re-raise until more than $20,000 is in the pot. Meredith, out of cash, is unable to call the latest raise. Under the strain, he collapses. The town physician, Joseph "Doc" Scully (Burgess Meredith), is called to care for the stricken man. Barely conscious, Meredith signals for his wife to play out the hand. Taking his seat, Mary asks, "How do you play this game?" You won't believe what follows.

In his last feature film role, Bickford acquits himself capably at the age of 76.

4. *The Plainsman* – 1936

Already covered under the films of Gary Cooper. Wild Bill Hickok[44] and Calamity Jane attempt to stop an Indian uprising that was started

---

[44] Wild Bill Hickok was another one of those western folk heroes whose real life was much different than the way he was portrayed in movies and on television. Real name James Butler Hickok, he was known for his skills as a farmer, vigilante, drover, teamster, wagon master, soldier, spy, scout, detective, lawman, gunfighter, and gambler. He was regarded as a liar by most of his contemporaries. Hickok was shot by a fellow card player – Jack McCall - and died in Deadwood, South Dakota in 1876 at the age of 39.

by mercenary white gun runners. Bickford plays John Lattimer, the greediest of all the gunrunners who is the front man for the sale of guns to the Native Americans. Charles Bickford at his meanest.

5. Duel in the Sun – 1946

This film is also covered under the movies of Gregory Peck. The film covers the star-crossed love affair between Lewt (Peck) and Pearl (Jennifer Jones). Bickford has a fairly small but key part in the film.

Offended when Lewt reneges on a promise to marry her, Pearl takes up with Sam Pierce (Bickford), a neighboring rancher who is smitten with her. She does not love him but says yes to his marriage proposal. Before they can get to the altar, however, Lewt picks a fight with Pierce in a saloon and guns him down. He insists that Pearl can belong only to him. Lewt thus becomes a wanted man for the remainder of the film.

Gregory Peck and Jennifer Jones in Duel in the Sun. Several of the characters were "smitten" with her, and I can see why.

Summary

Lanky supporting actor Charles Bickford was a strong presence as a character actor in a wide range of film genres, from westerns to dramas in particular. He even had a small part in one of my all-time favorite films, 1942's *Reap the Wild Wind*, in which he played the

Master of the Tyfib fishing boat, the guy who tries to grab lawyer Ray Milland and sell him to a whaling boat. The film was directed by Cecil B. DeMille and starred Paulette Goddard, Ray Milland, John Wayne, Raymond Massey, Robert Preston, Susan Hayward, and Lynne Overman, in addition to Bickford.

Like most of the supporting actors and villains, he also started on stage before going into films and also did a lot of television work throughout his career. A most deserving western villain.

John Wayne, Paulette Goddard, and Ray Milland in *Reap the Wild Wind* (1942)

And Now: My Favorite Westerns of that Era

I am not saying that these are the 12 best westerns of that era, just that they are my favorite westerns of that particular period of film making. Not really in order of preference, however; I liked all of them.

1. *The Searchers* – 1956

Simply one of the best westerns of all time, but not really well received by the public when it first appeared. John Wayne's character – Ethan Edwards – is a flawed one, bent on revenge against the Indians at all costs. He and nephew Jeffrey Hunter spend a good decade searching for the daughter of his brother, whose entire family - except for the one daughter – was massacred by Indians on their small Texas ranch. Beautiful scenery and top performances by people like Natalie Wood, Ward Bond, Vera Miles, and Hank Worden.

2. *Red River* – 1948

Black and white film based on the first cattle drive along the Chisholm Trail from Texas to Abilene, Kansas and all the conflicts between a middle-aged man – John Wayne – and his adopted son – Montgomery Clift. A superb supporting cast includes Walter Brennan, Joanne Dru, John Ireland, and Harry Carey. A great ending to a great western.

Nominated for Oscars for Best Writing and Best Film Editing.

3. *High Noon* - 1952

Perhaps Gary Cooper's best role as the retiring sheriff of a small western town. On his wedding day, Coop realizes he must face off once more against a killer he put in jail years before, Frank Miller, as well as the rest of his gang. He finds out that the townspeople he has served valiantly all these years have turned against him, for one reason or another. Gary Cooper shows real fear as he realizes he is on his own without any support. The film also stars Grace Kelly, Katy Jurado, Lloyd Bridges, Lon Chaney, Jr., Thomas Mitchell, and Harry Morgan. And who can forget the haunting melody of "Do Not Forsake Me Oh My Darling" sung by Tex Ritter throughout the film?

Won Oscars for Best Actor – Gary Cooper, of course – Best Film Editing, Best Music, and Best Original Song. Nominated for Best Picture, Best Director, and Best Writing, but did not win.

4. *Shane* – 1953

Alan Ladd's signature western role as a reformed gunman and drifter seeking a peaceful life who comes to a small Wyoming town and immediately gets involved in a range war with the old ranchers versus the new settlers. He comes to live with Joe Starrett (Van Heflin) and his wife Marian (Jean Arthur in her final big-screen role) and son Joey (Brandon De Wilde). I love the understated events in the movie; there is an obvious attraction between Shane and Marian yet nothing is ever brought to fruition; we know that Shane is probably a gunfighter but it is never overtly stated. Shane is slow to fight and avoids it at all costs. Plus, the ranchers are not really villains – they fought for the land they own and have a right to it, they are simply not willing to share it with the newcomers. When the ranchers fear they are losing out, they call in for reinforcements in the form of Jack Wilson (Jack Palance), a psychotic killer.

This film has a great supporting cast of western players, including Elisha Cook, Jr., Ben Johnson, Edgar Buchanan, Emile Meyer, John Dierkes, and Ellen Corby.

GOOD GUYS, BAD GUYS, AND SIDEKICKS IN WESTERN MOVIES

Previous page. Alan Ladd defends his friends – Van Heflin, Jean Arthur (in her final movie) and Brandon DeWilde – in Shane

5. *My Darling Clementine* - 1946

One of all-time favorite western legends – The Earps and Doc Holliday against the Clantons and their supporters – this might be the single best version of the tale. Henry Fonda as the stoic Wyatt Earp is great, and Victor Mature as his sometime friend Doc Holliday might even be better. Walter Brennan is the mean Ike Clanton, and Linda Darnell plays Doc's girlfriend, the vivacious Chihuahua.

But who is Clementine? Doc's girlfriend from back East, who comes to Tombstone to find out what the heck happened to him, and who adds to his woes because he no longer feels he deserves her.

> On April 9, 1965, screen beauty Linda Darnell was at the home of her former secretary, located in Glenview, Illinois. The house caught on fire in the early hours of the next morning and Darnell died that afternoon in Cook County Hospital in Chicago. She was only 41 at the time – very tragic.

6. *The Ox-Bow Incident* - 1943

This classic 1943 western film is focused on the dangers of vigilante justice. A local rancher's cattle are stolen and he is murdered. While the sheriff is out investigating his death, the townspeople decide to form a posse and find the killer or killers themselves. Two cowhands passing through – played by Henry Fonda and Harry Morgan – join the posse.

They come across Dana Andrews and the other two members of his party and quickly decide they are the murderers, despite Andrews' having a legitimate bill of sale for the cattle and insisting that he knew nothing about the murder. Despite the protests of a small group of the posse – who want to bring the three men back to justice and face trial – the majority are bent on hanging them right then and there.

The film examines what happens when what seems to be a normal group of men – and one woman, played by Jane Darwell – lose all sense of reason and become a vigilante mob. A good performance by Henry Fonda and an even better one by Dana Andrews, trying to plead for his life against an angry mob bent on revenge.

Nominated for an Oscar for Best Picture but did not win.

7. *Bad Day at Black Rock* - 1955

A great Spencer Tracy film about a WWII veteran (Tracy) who travels to a small western town to give a medal to the father of a Japanese-American soldier who saved his life. When he finds that the soldier is dead under mysterious circumstances and no one wants to provide any information, he decides to stay in town and investigate himself. Much to the chagrin of Robert Ryan, Ernest Borgnine, Anne Francis, and Lee Marvin, and much to the delight of Walter Brennan and – to a certain extent – ineffectual sheriff Dean Jagger.

Tracy's performance as the slow-to-burn but determined one-armed veteran is outstanding, and the rest of the cast is good also. Racial prejudice is showcased, but this time it is against Asians rather than Native Americans as in most westerns. The film also demonstrates how one individual – even one with only one arm – can make a difference (and also beat the stuffing out of a bully like Ernest Borgnine!) And you have never seen a worse-looking western town than Black Rock.

Bad Day at Black Rock was nominated for three Oscars, including a Best Actor Oscar for Spencer Tracy (his fifth), as well as Best Director and Best Writing. .

8. *Stagecoach* - 1939

As already discussed, this is the film that made John Wayne a star, and rightly so. While he is the central figure in the story, the beauty of this film is its ensemble cast of characters, all of whom have roughly the same size part in this film. While Wayne and Claire Trevor are viewed somewhat as outcasts by the rest of the traveling party – he is a criminal, she is a prostitute – they soon form a bond that leads the viewer to hope for a better life for the two of them in the future.

Stagecoach won Oscars for Best Supporting Actor – Thomas Mitchell – and Best Musical Scoring. It was nominated for Best Black and White Cinematography, Best Film Editing, and Best Art Direction.

9. *Winchester 73* – **1950**

Like all the films in this group, Winchester 73 has already been discussed – in this case, under the films of James Stewart and also Dan Duryea. The action follows the journey of the prized rifle – won by Stewart in a shooting contest but then stolen from him – through different owners to its being reunited with Stewart at the end of the film. Lots of tension, and two equally nasty villains – Duryea and Stephen McNally - and Shelley Winters as the damsel in distress.

10. *The Man Who Shot Liberty Valance* - **1962**

I have already discussed this film under the films of both James Stewart and John Wayne. The pairing of Wayne and Stewart is a stroke of genius; Wayne plays the outgoing, confident, but flawed hero, while Stewart is the morally superior tenderfoot. Lee Marvin is just about as mean and nasty a villain as you will ever see, and the conclusion tells you who really shot Liberty Valance. As the film says, "When the legend becomes fact, print the legend."

The film was nominated for one Oscar, Best Costume Design for a black and white film.

11. *3:10 To Yuma* - **1957**

The 1957 version of this movie is one of my favorites for a couple of reasons: The stellar performance of Van Heflin as the husband and father who is trying to make a go of it with land that is practically worthless, and especially the work of Glenn Ford (Ben Wade) as the seemingly nice-guy villain who is really a cold-blooded killer. Heflin accepts a huge reward for volunteering to take Ford to the nearest town to board the train to Yuma, with Ford's gang, led by Richard Jaeckel, in hot pursuit. Ford attempts to get Heflin to release him, promising to pay him the same amount and keep him alive, but Heflin is a man of his word. The tension in this film builds to a thrilling conclusion.

Ford could have easily been nominated for an Oscar but was not. He gave a terrific performance, however.

12. *The Gunfighter* – 1950

A reformed Gunfighter, Jimmy Ringo, (Why are so many western bad guys and gunmen named Ringo?) is on his way to a sleepy town in the hope of a reunion with his estranged sweetheart and their young son whom he has never seen. On arrival, a chance meeting with some old friends including the town's Marshal gives the repentant Jimmy some hope for a brighter future. But as always Jimmy's reputation has already cast its shadow, this time in the form of three vengeful cowboys hot on his trail and a local gunslinger hoping to use Jimmy to make a name for himself. With a showdown looming, the town is soon in a frenzy as news of Jimmy's arrival spreads. His movements are restricted to the saloon while a secret meeting with his son can be arranged, giving him ideas of a long term reunion with his family far removed from his wild past. But is it meant to be?

Gregory Peck gives a beautiful performance as the weary gunfighter who realizes that no matter how fast you are, there is always someone who is faster.

The *Gunfighter* was nominated for one Oscar, for best writing.

GOOD GUYS, BAD GUYS, AND SIDEKICKS IN WESTERN MOVIES

ACKNOWLEDGMENTS

As in my book on *Forgotten Movie Stars of the 30's, 40's, and 50's*, I acknowledge those responsible for keeping classic movies of that era alive – most notably, Turner Classic Movies and The Western Channel on STARZ. I also acknowledge the following four sources:
1. Wikipedia
2. The International Movie Data Base – IMDB
3. www.fanpix.net
4. Commons.wikimedia.org – for photos in the public domain

NOTES

I have attempted to use italics to identify movies and quotes to identify television shows and plays, but there might be an occasional inconsistency.

THANKS

Many thanks to the following three individuals for proofreading my book and catching some errors: Pat Koca, Bill Kolasinski, and Don Wisowaty.

ABOUT THE AUTHOR

Gary Koca has had a love of old movies for as far back as he can remember. Professionally, he worked in human resources for 42 years, either as a Federal government employee or contractor. During that time, he wrote hundreds of position papers, proposals, articles for journals, letters, and many other written products. Now retired and able to devote more time to writing about his two favorite topics – baseball and old movies from the 1930's, 40's, and 50's - his major character flaw is being a life-long fan of the Chicago Cubs. Gary is married with two daughters and four grandchildren and lives in suburban Chicago and Central Florida.

His previous books include *Forgotten Movie Stars of the 30s, 40s, and 50s*, (2013) and *Great Chicago Cub Baseball Players Since 1876* (2015). Both are available on www.Amazon.com.

Printed in Great Britain
by Amazon